Family money
matters

How to run your family
finances to God's glory

INCLUDES FREE
BUDGET WORKSHEET
DOWNLOAD

Lifestyle

yOne

SECURE

BROKE

IN DEBT

BANKRUPT

John Temple

"I am thankful for this book."
—Paul David Tripp, author
of *Age of Opportunity*

© Day One Publications 2010
First printed 2010

ISBN 978–1–84625–203–7

British Library Cataloguing in Publication Data available

Unless otherwise indicated, Scripture quotations are from **The Holy Bible, English Standard Version (ESV)**, copyright © 2001 by Crossway Bibles, a division of Good News Publishers. Used by permission. All rights reserved.

Published by Day One Publications
Ryelands Road, Leominster, HR6 8NZ
☎ 01568 613 740 FAX 01568 611 473
email—sales@dayone.co.uk
web site—www.dayone.co.uk
North American—e-mail—sales@dayonebookstore.com
North American—web site—www.dayonebookstore.com

Cover design by Wayne McMaster
Printed by Thomson Litho, East Kilbride

I am thankful for John Temple's book. Here is a man who loves God, loves the wisdom of the Word and is zealous to help you build a biblical worldview of your money and how you use it. What is even better is that he will not only challenge the motives of your heart and tell you how to think, he will also tell you what to do.

Paul David Tripp, member of pastoral team, Tenth Presbyterian Church, Philadelphia, and author of Age of Opportunity

Did you ever long for a simple, short, wise guide from a Christian perspective on how to handle family finances? John Temple has provided it in Family Money Matters, *which covers the basics of biblical views on stewardship, heart-motivation, and generosity, as well as practical advice about living within your means, establishing a family budget, and addressing questions related to investments, insurance, debt, and much more. This little book is packed full of biblical principles and practicalities from a brother who lives what he writes.*

Joel R. Beeke, President of Puritan Reformed Theological Seminary, Grand Rapids, Michigan, USA

About the author

D r. John Temple has spent a lifetime exploring ways of applying the Bible to everyday life, including domestic finances. John holds a Ph.D. from King's College, London, and an AEP (MBA equivalent) from the University of South Africa. He has spent most of his life in top management, the last thirteen years of his fulltime career as CEO of an international group. Born and raised in South Africa, he and his wife, Yvonne, now live in the New Forest, England, but they spend a great deal of time in the USA, where three of their four children and their families live. John and Yvonne raised their children in line with the principles outlined in this book, and they in turn are using them to raise their children.

Here is what John and Yvonne's children say:

"I started adulthood with no emotional scars, but with self-confidence, a biblical worldview, the ability to figure things out for myself, money-management skills and so much more."

Meryl-Ann (USA), computer programmer, entrepreneur, home-educator and mother of four

"I have had the privilege of watching my parents over forty-something years live out the principles outlined in this book. It is one thing to pen words and quite another to consistently put them into practice."

Lynne (USA), Occupational Therapist, manager and mother of two

"Buy it, read it, implement the principles! I thank God I was taught these principles from when I was young and so today my family is debt-free—we are now teaching our children the same lessons."

David (USA), accountant, president of a computer company and father of five

"To learn about finance you can do at university, to learn about how to handle money as a Christian, you need to be taught at home. I learned it at home and this book will help you teach your children the same principles."

Peter (London), actuary, CEO of a large re-insurance company and father of three

Contents

Acknowledgments

I am grateful to God for the way he has blessed my family in all the material and spiritual benefits that we enjoy. We seek to remember his greatness and generosity in our daily prayers.

I am grateful to Paul David Tripp for his thought-provoking Foreword. As it gives a succinct summary of what I endeavor to say, I do trust that readers will read beyond it!

I am also grateful to my children, who had to grow up while my wife and I tried to discover the biblical way of doing things. Sadly, we often failed, but we are grateful to God for his grace in overruling where we failed.

Finally, my thanks go to Suzanne Mitchell, for editing the book with obvious professionalism.

I am by no means an expert in money and finances but there are a few things I know: the way you use your resources is always an indicator of what really does rule your heart; you use your money in pursuit of what is of value to you; you use your money for that which gives you meaning and purpose; your use of money is an expression of what gives you identity and that inner sense of well-being; and you simply can't separate the use of money and worship.

The debt load of the average member of the Body of Christ is a scandal. We are a church in debt, and the debt we carry seriously constricts our ability to resource God's kingdom work around the world. The statistics say that 80 percent of the offerings on a typical Sunday are given by 20 percent of those attending. These realities force us to consider why we are in such debt. Could it be that many Christians are using money in a way which was never intended by God? Could it be that we have bought the world's value system? Could it be that our debt is a sad indicator of what we really love and functionally worship?

When it comes to money, we have tended to set up a false spiritual/secular dichotomy. Budgets, economics, business, finances, sales, negotiations, contracts, debt, interest, and so on, get relegated to the "secular" dimension of our lives. Preachers are reticent about talking too much about money, and the church seems all too silent on the topic. The fact is that all of life is spiritual, including money. Your stewardship of the resources you have been given is a principle indicator of the character and quality of your relationship with God.

The resources (financial and otherwise) you have been given don't actually belong to you. All that you are and have belongs to the Lord. Here is what your financial life is about. You have been chosen to be one of the Lord's stewards and have been entrusted with a certain portion of his riches to invest in a way that provides for you and those he has placed in your care, that helps support his work on earth, and that ultimately gives him glory. When you give a tithe or offering, you aren't giving of what is yours to the Lord; no, you are returning what already belongs to the Lord for the work of his kingdom.

Many Christians are not financially trained and, therefore, not financially wise. Many are just "winging it" when it comes to their finances. They don't know how to budget. They aren't committed to saving. They haven't considered the implications of their debt. They live hand to mouth and hope it keeps working, and they pass this system of unplanned and reactive economics down to the next generation.

When to comes to finances, many Christians simply don't take the Fall of the world seriously. We live in a world that has been significantly damaged by sin. It simply does not operate as God intended. Because these Christians don't take the Fall seriously, when it comes to their money, they live with unrealistic dreams and are naïve when faced with the seduction of temptation. They don't recognize the danger of the magazine, the salesperson and the mall. They don't realize that they are daily being enticed to serve false gods with their money, and because they don't, they use their money in ways they shouldn't and for things that will never fulfill the cravings of their hearts.

So I am thankful for John Temple's book. Here is a man who loves God, loves the wisdom of the Word and is zealous to help you build a biblical worldview of your money and how you use it. What is even better is that he will not only challenge the motives of your heart and tell you how to think, he will also tell you what to do. Because of this, John Temple's voice is a welcome one in a conversation about things we simply don't talk about enough.

Paul David Tripp

Introduction

My wife and I set up our first home in North London. I was a postgraduate international student on a scholarship and was only permitted to work for a limited number of hours each week. My wife was not permitted to work at all. We were as poor as the proverbial church mouse. We took in another postgraduate student as a lodger, which, in effect enabled my wife to earn some income. We also lived as frugally as we could but, notwithstanding all these efforts, by the time I had completed my Ph.D. we had built up a substantial student loan. On our return to South Africa (which was then home) we were faced with new challenges. Our second daughter was on the way, and we needed a home, furniture, a car and so on. We tried to avoid further debt by buying a sound but elderly car, and I made a lot of our furniture and painted our first house. All to no avail; our debts increased. We found that we were borrowing to pay the interest on what we had already borrowed! Does this sound familiar?

I am giving this background because I think it illustrates a situation with which many can identify. How do we avoid these situations, and, if we are in one, how do we get out of it?

This book will deal with these issues on a very practical level, but, as always, we must establish the biblical principles which will guide us as we search for solutions. However, even before we do that, it is worth looking at those parts of secular economics which govern so much of our lives. We will do this in the next chapter in order to contrast biblical principles with the underlying assumptions of secular thinking to which we easily succumb.

No doubt readers will want to know how my wife and I got out of our financial troubles. Quite simply by following the biblical pattern of work, earn, live carefully, pay off debts, and then never spend more than you can afford, all the while paying a minimum of 10 percent to the Lord's work. My wife and I started sideline businesses, first giving private mathematics lessons and then going into property development. We quickly worked our way out of trouble. Note that Paul, when writing to the Ephesians, taught that we should go even further: "Let the thief no longer steal, but rather let him labor, doing honest work with his own hands, so that he may have something *to share* with anyone in need" (Eph. 4:28[1]). Part of our motivation to earn as much as we can is to be able to share, not to indulge ourselves in selfish ways.

Sound economics also requires that you are paid what you earn, or, put differently, that you deliver real value for the money that you are paid. A contributing part of the financial crisis of the past few years was the enormous amounts paid to people in the financial sector when they had, in fact, failed. It was reported that in 2008 (in the midst of the crisis), three financiers in New York together received bonuses of $1 billion. In the UK some £18 billion (about $30 billion) was paid in bonuses to people in the City. Could they possibly have earned this when almost the entire industry failed? But the problem is widespread. I am constantly amazed at the low output I see from workers in almost every trade or profession. Put simply, many people at every level are overpaid for their output.

In the next chapter we see that the *secular* economic order is to borrow, spend, then earn, and then borrow more, spend more and so on. Christians are to live in such a way that our lives demonstrate different values from those of our secular neighbors, colleagues and friends. This is one area where we can truly be different. We must not worship the same idols the world worships, namely those of materialism, consumption and entertainment. There is, however, a fine line because, as I will say repeatedly, God intends us to enjoy him *and all that he has graciously given us* (see 1 Tim. 6:17b). We must also show our neighbors that we are not "weird" but "normal" in all matters which are morally acceptable. So we can live in decent homes, drive good cars, dress in respectable clothing, go on vacation and so on. But we do not make these high-priority items in our budgets (making them idols), and we certainly do not get into debt for most of them.

This book may seem to assume that you are either part of a typical family consisting of father and mother with some children, or in the process of building a family. However, I recognize that many readers will be single or single parents. All of the principles still apply.

The book does assume that you are a follower of Jesus Christ and that you want to pursue the principles of finance as set out in the Bible. But perhaps you have never become a true follower of Christ, even if you call yourself "Christian." It is not difficult to commit yourself to the Lord. When Paul was asked what we have to do to be saved, his answer was, "Believe in the Lord Jesus, and you will be saved ..." (Acts 16:31). It is impossible to believe in Jesus without believing what he came to do. God is angry with us because we are sinners, and he demands punishment. Jesus took our place, taking the punishment due to us when he died on the cross. We therefore need to repent (i.e. turn away from our sin). Space does not allow me to pursue this subject fully but I recommend *Where Do We Go from Here?* by John Blanchard and *Reach Out For Him* by Gary Benfold for those who want to find out more.[2]

I encourage all readers to make an effort to pursue biblical principles in *all* aspects of their home lives. If you have young children in your home, make this a companion book to Ted Tripp's *Shepherding a Child's Heart*;[3] if you have teenage children, add Paul Tripp's *Age of Opportunity*.[4] In both cases, read *Family Driven Faith* by Voddie Baucham.[5]

Finally, this is not a detailed "how to" book that gives precise and detailed procedures or programs for doing things; rather it aims to teach understanding of the *principles* of home finance so that readers can make sound decisions and develop their own solutions. For readers who want more help, I have produced MS Excel spreadsheets for all the budgets given in the book. They can be obtained from the Day One Web site.[6] Readers who want an even more detailed "road map" should consult the Web sites of Crown Ministries, Dave Ramsey or Mint.[7]

Notes

1 All emphasis within Scripture quotations is the author's.

2 **John Blanchard,** *Where Do We Go from Here?* (Darlington: Evangelical Press, 2008); **Gary Benfold,** *Reach Out For Him: Knowing the Unknown God* (Leominster: Day One, 2006).

3 **Ted Tripp,** *Shepherding a Child's Heart: Parent's Handbook* (Wapwallopen, PA: Shepherd Press, 2001).

4 **Paul Tripp,** *Age of Opportunity: A Biblical Guide to Parenting Teens* (Phillipsburg, NJ: P&R, 2001).

5 **Voddie Baucham Jr.,** *Family Driven Faith: Doing What it Takes to Raise Sons and Daughters Who Walk with God* (Wheaton, IL: Crossway, 2007). Dr. Baucham has written several other useful books on the family.

6 US readers should visit dayonebookstore.com; UK readers should visit dayone.co.uk. Find the page for this book (you can search for it by title or by ISBN; if using the ISBN, type 9781846252037 into the Search box). There will be links from this page to all the MS Excel spreadsheets mentioned in this book.

7 Visit: crownmoneymap.org; daveramsey.com; mint.com (I have no association or interest in any of these organizations). I also recommend **Howard Dayton,** *Your Money Map: A Proven 7-Step Guide to True Financial Freedom* (Chicago: Moody, 2006) and **Larry Burkett,** *Family Financial Workbook* (Chicago: Moody, 2000).

The world's view of money

I am writing this book in the midst of the economic upheavals of 2007 to 2010. This period has been characterized by massive government and private debt, low business confidence, recession, increased joblessness, and the failure of banks and other supposedly strong companies. How did the world get into such a mess? In a nutshell, it came about through unrestrained greed. Greed practiced by consumers with an ever-increasing desire for material possessions, services and leisure. Greed practiced by bankers and financial executives who capitalized on the greed of their customers. Indeed, greed was encouraged by most Western governments. Let me explain in more detail.

Western economies are largely "consumer-led." This means that people are encouraged to spend, spend and spend some more, whether what they buy is necessary or simply for their enjoyment. This expenditure creates "demand" which is provided by an ever-increasing workforce that works to fulfill the "wants" (over and above the "needs") of the consumers. The outcome is apparent economic growth. Standards of living also increase due to the ever-increasing spiral of better products and more sophisticated services. Improvements in living standards (with some adverse consequences) also come through technology. Consider your own life. What sort of car did you drive ten years ago? What features were standard? What camera did you use? How many pixels did it have? How did you record videos, music and photos? Compare these items with what you use today. Did you ever think that early in the twenty-first century you would be able to make "free" video telephone calls around the globe? How much *more* do you spend today on leisure, vacations, entertainment and other nonessential items? Let me be clear: there is nothing intrinsically wrong with a rising standard of living, and all these items are given by "… God, who richly provides us with everything to enjoy" (1 Tim. 6:17; the context of this verse is important, however. It is not urging unrestrained indulgence). Rising living standards are legitimate if generated by improved technology or increased productivity. The latter means that more goods and services are obtained from the same resources, or, more particularly, through the same labor. It may be accomplished through harder work or longer hours, as well as through improved production technology and the elimination of non-productive jobs. However, if *lower* productivity (averaged over the nation) nullifies the impact of all these positive factors, the rate of inflation rises and no net gain is achieved by technology or anything else. Organized labor tends to demand shorter working hours, more time off and generally reduced pressure, tending toward *lower real national productivity*. At the same time, demand for all sorts of goods and services (much of it nonessential) increases through high-pressure advertising. This is the basis of the consumer-led economy. The entire edifice is finely balanced and can easily be toppled, as we have seen over the past few years.

What happens when consumers demand more than can be justified in terms of productivity gains? "Real incomes" (i.e. income after inflation) cannot then rise fast enough to overcome the effects of inflation. If this effect is added to the ever-increasing desire to live a "better life," people are forced to borrow, getting deeper and deeper into debt. This is known as the "fairy economy" and it suits everyone—for a while, anyway. The banks create an ever-increasing array of debt products which generate ever-increasing "paper" profits for the banks. Bank executives then earn ludicrous bonuses, which encourage them to find more ways of lending more money to more people, most of whom cannot repay the loans!

Consider some of the facts. Credit cards are issued to all and sundry with scant regard for the creditworthiness of the customers. Interest rates on these cards are nothing short of usury, never less than about 15 percent per annum (p.a.) but often approaching 30 percent. To this must be added an array of "fees" for late payments, over-limit usage and so on. To make matters worse, most credit cards require only a minimum monthly payment of 5–10 percent of the outstanding balance. Why? Because this creates ever-increasing debt. We could cite examples of credit being granted irresponsibly for the purchase of cars, furniture and other consumer goods. In short, *living in debt has become an acceptable way of life in our culture*.

Consider the mortgage market. Prospective home owners have sometimes been encouraged to obtain mortgages which exceeded the value of the properties, even before the value of houses fell. Often the repayments are also beyond the ability of the borrowers. These irresponsible loans created the "sub-prime" mortgage crisis of 2007 and 2008—the so-called "toxic" debt. This is not a minor problem; the volume of this debt runs into an estimated $6 trillion around the Western world.

Companies may be forced, through governance rules and shareholder concern, to limit their borrowings. But most companies are under pressure to show ever-increasing "earnings per share" (also referred to as EPS). One method of achieving a rising EPS without changing the basic performance of the company is through what is known as "gearing" or "leverage," in which a company finances its operations through *more* debt and *less* share capital. This means that the earnings are spread over fewer shares, giving rise to higher "earnings per share." In all the years I have been in control of companies, I have refused debt as a *permanent* means of finance because it tends to distort the underlying capability of the company and increases risk. On a superficial analysis, my EPS often looked inferior to those of my competitors and attracted criticism. So be it.

Governments are no different. Democratic governments are always in a dilemma. In order to get elected, they promise more and more benefits to voters. Governments obtain their income from taxes so they have to be cautious about telling the same voters that they will increase their taxes to pay for all these promises. If anyone points out that future taxes are bound to increase to pay for today's handouts, the standard answer is that the government will find ways of taxing "the rich" or of closing the tax "loopholes" employed by the rich. Simple arithmetic will usually demonstrate that there are simply neither enough "rich," nor sufficient loopholes, to get the sort of income that is needed. The middle-income group usually ends up bearing the brunt of the increase, but even this group has a limited capacity. So governments do what everyone else does. They borrow.

The US national debt (i.e. the government's debt) was about 60 percent of the nation's wealth as measured by the so-called gross domestic product (GDP) at the end of 2007 but will reach some 94 percent of GDP ($14 trillion) by 2010, according to the US Budget[1] for 2010/11. The last time it reached these levels was directly after World War 2. In the UK, at the beginning of 2008 the national debt was below 40 percent of GDP. This percentage is considered undesirable but "acceptable," and is below the EU's threshold of 60 percent. After all, it has been higher; for example, after World War 2. In addition, the UK government underwrites the private finance initiatives (PFI) for capital projects and is also committed to paying pensions, which liability has a present value but is not included in the national debt. Without getting too deeply into economic definitions, we can say that these are, in effect, all government debt. If we then add the refinancing of several large banks and the stimulation of the economy, this figure for national debt goes up substantially and, according to many economists, will rise to 100 percent of GDP by the end of 2010. Other Western nations are no different. Germany was at 68 percent; Italy, 100 percent; and Japan, 194 percent. Most governments of the Western world have debt of 50–200 percent GDP. No one knows what a reasonable ratio might be, but surely we must be close to the limit. It is worth noting that many economists agree that the national debt is ideally close to zero; US President Jackson (1767–1845) managed to reduce the US national debt to a mere $33,000 when he left office (the lowest in the history of the USA).

Again, without getting into definitions of private debt, let me illustrate the size of the problem facing families today. In the USA, in 2008, the aggregate debt of private people amounted to nearly five times the GDP; in the UK, it amounted to at least three times the GDP! For at least a decade, leading economists have warned that a national private debt of over twice the GDP will place the entire world economy at risk. If we combined all private debt in 2008 and divided it by the number of families in the USA or Great Britain, we would arrive at the alarming result that, on average, each US family would owe about $700,000, and each British family about £400,000. Similar levels apply to other Western nations. To continue with these numbers requires "confidence" that the debt will be repaid, even though common sense says that there is no chance of everyone repaying these debts within their lifetimes. Until now, the assumption was that inflation in the housing market would help repay these debts. When house prices began to fall, the rest was inevitable.

None of us needs be an economist to grasp that this "paper" economy cannot be sustained. Yet the "solution" proposed by all governments so far is to get their economies rolling by *increasing* debt even more. Indeed, one of the conditions attached to the bank bail-out offered by the British government in 2008 was that the banks return to lending at the 2007 levels. These are the very levels that got the economy into trouble in the first place! Why do the governments do this, then? Because secular economists and governments cannot conceive of an economy free from debt. The problem, however, is deeper because the world has learned to depend not only on debt, but on an *increasing level of debt* to fund increasing consumer demand and, with it, imaginary economic growth. Most governments are in the position that I got into as described in the Introduction: they are borrowing *to pay the interest on their debt.* In the USA the interest bill on government debt will be some $164 billion by 2010, and in the UK it will rise during 2009/10 to well over £60 billion p.a. At the time of writing, the UK's Labour government has claimed that increasing tax on the "rich" (those with incomes of over £150,000 p.a. and representing just 1 percent of taxpayers) will raise £7 billion p.a. to help pay for this interest and higher debt. This is doubtful, but even if it does occur, it hardly makes a dent in the increased interest alone!

It is interesting to note what the Archbishop of Canterbury, Dr. Rowan Williams, had to say in December 2008 on BBC Radio 4 when he was asked to comment on whether increased spending (based on debt) was the right way to tackle the downturn. He said, "… it seems a little bit like the addict returning to the drug. When the Bible uses the word 'repentance,' it doesn't just mean beating your breast, it means getting a new perspective, and that is perhaps what we are shrinking away from." The archbishop added, "It is about what is sustainable in the long term and if this is going to drive us back into the same spin, I do not think that is going to help us."[2] Williams is not an economist but he could see the *moral* implications of avoiding the real solution. At the heart of the problem is the desire in our secular culture for *instant gratification.* We do not want to save before we buy. The oft-repeated slogan of the debt-based consumer society is "buy now, pay later."

To be sure, the economy is vastly more complex than is indicated by the above few paragraphs. The causes of today's economic troubles are also due to factors more complex than debt or greed alone (e.g. government's abdication from regulation and policing of the financial markets). I raise these issues because they are major cultural contributors to *family* economic woes and set the scene for a biblical consideration of how things *ought to be*. I will resist the temptation of proposing possible remedies for the financial crisis, but will predict some of the actions of governments, as this will have a bearing on some of the matters I raise in subsequent chapters. No government is likely to address the real issues apart from a restoration of financial regulations. These should be welcomed because the first role of government is to protect its people. This implies policing *every* activity, including banking. Instead, however, governments will print money. In the UK this is euphemistically referred to as "quantitative easing"—whatever that may mean! At least the Zimbabweans called it by its correct name: "printing money." Printing money reduces the value of all currency-denominated assets, including the so-called "toxic debt." The disadvantage is that it reduces the value of *all* such assets, including savings. Overall it reduces the *value* of our currency, which means that we will have to pay more to get the same goods—another way of describing inflation. For a real taste of the ultimate outcome of printing money, simply look at Zimbabwe. No doubt no Western nation will go to the same extreme, but the results will still be serious, especially for people on fixed incomes, such as pensioners. It seems odd that, in a world calling continuously for "social justice," most people seem, in my view, to be content to let pensioners bear the brunt of the solution. The other likely outcome of the economic policies of Western governments will be to increase the power of the nations that do have money, largely China and nations in the Middle East. Western governments seem to be overlooking this rather obvious vulnerability. If only they would read Proverbs 22:7: "The rich rules over the poor, and the borrower is the slave of the lender." At the G20 summit in Pittsburgh in September 2009 it was acknowledged that China and India were to be given more influence. The Middle East will be next. Think about the consequences of this as far as the spread of the gospel is concerned.

May we heed the advice of Paul in our approach to financial matters, namely that we should "... not be conformed to this world, but be transformed by the renewal of your mind, that by testing you may discern what is the will of God, what is good and acceptable and perfect" (Rom. 12:2). He indicated at least some of that "good and acceptable and perfect" will of God when he said, "Now there is great gain in godliness with contentment ..." (1 Tim. 6:6).

Notes

1 See: usgovernmentspending.com.
2 Quoted by **Martin Beckford,** "Archbishop of Canterbury: Gordon Brown's Recovery Plan Like 'Addict Returning to Drug,'" December 18, 2008, at: telegraph.co.uk.

Biblical considerations

We have looked at some of the key elements of the economic culture in which we live, summarized as consuming and enjoying ourselves *now* through increased debt fuelled by greed. This is sometimes referred to as "materialism," "hedonism" or "the pursuit of things" and "fun." As Christians, it is all too easy simply to absorb these values of our culture and to see them as normal and therefore acceptable. The problem is that, even fifty years ago, these values were *not normal*, even to non-Christians. They were even less normal 100 or 150 years ago. Secular culture moves with the times. If we simply follow what everyone else is doing we may (probably will) cross a biblical boundary. Christians may follow secular culture in all matters which are "neutral"— i.e. do not contradict any biblical principle—but we must question all our actions in the light of biblical teaching. The consumer-led economy is the logical outcome of a worldview which teaches that by chance we came from apes, live meaningless lives and will end up nowhere. Under these circumstances, consuming and enjoying goods ("having fun") is all the world has to offer. "Let us eat and drink, for tomorrow we die" (Isa. 22:13). To have fun *now* requires debt for most of us.

This is not the place to give a comprehensive review of biblical economics (for more of this, see my book *Be Successful, Be Spiritual*[1]), so I have restricted what I say to those elements which affect our family finances and are in contrast to the secular worldview described above.

In the chapters which follow I will be dealing with the very practical financial issues which we all face almost on a daily basis. In most situations we will not have any direct biblical guidance, so we will need to keep the biblical principles and boundaries uppermost in our minds and determine how to apply them to our practical decisions.

Stewardship

We start where the Bible starts, in Genesis. God delegated to us the responsibility of looking after his creation. This is stewardship. It is part of being made in his image and is a truly humbling thought. God judged all that he had created to be "good" and then left us to care for it. He judged that we possess enough of his attributes to do the job. Consider the early account from creation: "The LORD God took the man and put him in the garden of Eden to work it and keep it" (Gen. 2:15). The consequence of this is that everything on earth is on loan to us. We do not deserve any of it, and whatever use we make of it is part of God's grace. Even our hard work (which is good) is not the only reason why we accumulate wealth. See what the Bible says: "Beware lest you say in your heart, 'My power and the might of my hand have gotten me this wealth.' You shall remember the LORD your God, for it is *he who gives* you power to get wealth, that he may confirm his covenant that he swore to your fathers, as it is this day" (Deut. 8:17–18). We are to see all that we "own" or earn in this light.

Stewardship in the Bible literally means "management of a household" (or "the law over the house"), in much the same way in which the slave Joseph managed the home of Potiphar. Just as a slave owned none of the things that he or she managed, so we own nothing. It can all be swept away in an instant. Consider Job, a wealthy man. For reasons unrelated to *his* behavior, he lost everything so that God could prove a point before the watching hosts of heaven. God is entitled to do this because he is the Creator and Ruler of the universe.

Stewards were mostly slaves in New Testament times, although they were sometimes referred to as "servants." We should all see ourselves as "servants," however influential or wealthy we may be.

Stewardship applies to our management of church, mission or business affairs, but it also applies to *our own finances* and *our own possessions.* Most of us are probably good stewards of that portion of our income that we give to the Lord (say the 10 percent). But are we good stewards of the other 90 percent? We are always to remember that that 90 percent is also "on loan" to us and to treat everything in this light. Stewardship implies not wasting anything. Certainly not money.

Jesus also taught that we are stewards of all our resources and will be called to account for how we protect and develop them (see Luke 16:1–2). The parable of the talents (Matt. 25:14–30) is equally challenging, requiring us to *develop* our talents in addition to preserving them. While these principles apply to all resources, they are illustrated by Jesus using financial examples.

Motives

Most of us would answer the question, "What is the chief end of man?" with at least part of the correct answer, namely, "to glorify God." However, do we *live* this way? Why do we strive to have more, to live better lives and to have "fun"? James gave the answer:

What causes quarrels and what causes fights among you? Is it not this, that your passions are at war within you? You desire and do not have, so you murder. You covet and cannot obtain, so you fight and quarrel. You do not have, because you do not ask. You ask and do not receive, because you ask wrongly, to spend it on your passions.

(James 4:1–3)

Paul equally condemns our age when he says, "But understand this, that in the last days there will come times of difficulty. For people will be lovers of self, *lovers of money … without self-control …* not loving good, treacherous, reckless, swollen with conceit, *lovers of pleasure* rather than lovers of God …" (2 Tim. 3:1–4). Elsewhere he says, "For the *love* of money is a root of all kinds of evils" (1 Tim. 6:10).

If we go on to answer the balance of the question posed above, we would add, "and to enjoy him [God] forever." The point is that our enjoyment is to be found *in God*, not in indulging our passions. The world would answer, "and to enjoy *ourselves* forever," which is hedonism. As Christians we need to be proactive in resisting the temptation to follow the world and in obeying God's laws instead. We must therefore discover what these laws are.

May we use money and possessions as a measure of success in a person's life? To a certain extent it is not wrong to do so, although it is only one measure among many other more important outcomes in life. Nevertheless, there is no virtue in failure, and if we live and work correctly we may well make money. The first fourteen verses of Deuteronomy 28 set out God's promises, which can be summarized by the following extracts: "And if you faithfully obey the voice of the LORD your God, being careful to do all his commandments that I command you today, the LORD your God will set you high above all the nations of the earth … And the LORD will make you abound in prosperity …" (Deut. 28:1, 11). The remainder of the chapter sets out curses which are the opposite of the blessings and result from a failure to observe God's commands. God reminded them that, when they settled down, they should "remember the LORD your God, for it is he who gives you power to get wealth" (Deut. 8:18). The power to get wealth comes with a condition: "remember the LORD your God." These verses were given to the Old Testament nation of Israel and cannot be applied to individual Christians today. But in general, as the new Israel, we will enjoy God's gifts as we live by his Word. The problem is that we *all too readily convert his blessings into idols*. We must worship *God* so that our motivation will be to point people to him and to promote his glory, not to boast in our prosperity. Paul gave us tangible ways in which we can glorify God with possessions and money. This is more fully described below but can be summarized as: "to be rich in good works, to be generous and ready to share" (1 Tim. 6:18).

Greed

The underlying assumption of most pay and incentive schemes operating in the West is that people can be motivated by greed. This was most evident in the banking collapses of 2008/09. We are all caught up in this culture. This book started out showing how greed has been a major factor in causing the near collapse of our economic system. As Christians we can hardly escape the temptations of greed. But escape it we must. Listen to what Jesus had to say: "Woe to you, scribes and Pharisees, hypocrites! For you clean the outside of the cup and the plate, but inside they are full of *greed and self-indulgence*" (Matt. 23:25). Now listen to Peter: "They have hearts trained in greed. Accursed children!" (2 Peter 2:14). Greed is a form of idolatry, for it is worship of material things rather than our God. It will ruin our spiritual lives if we do not get it under control. It is roundly condemned in the Bible. Instead, we are to learn Paul's lesson: "I have learned in whatever situation I am to be content" (Phil. 4:11); and the lesson of Proverbs 30:8: "give me neither poverty nor riches; feed me with the food that is needful for me."

How do we overcome greed? In the next section I deal with what may appear to be a surprising antidote. For a more detailed look at this subject, I recommend *Beyond Greed* by Brian Rosner.[2]

Generosity

One aspect of the fruit of the Spirit is self-control (Gal. 5:23). This grace is not emphasized nearly enough and is practiced even less. Our lack of self-control causes us to succumb to many temptations, especially the respectable sins of overindulgence and greed. Consider God's nature. He is the supreme example of self-control. We often read in the Bible of God's wrath and his threat of punishing mankind, but mostly we read of his restraint. Just because he *can* punish and destroy us all, it does not result in him always *doing* so. In fact, he was prepared to send his beloved Son to die for our sins rather than destroy us all. God restrained himself by placing his righteousness (and love of us) above his love for his own beloved Son. Yet we seem to believe that whatever we *can* do, we *may* do. Just because we *can* afford something, we believe that we are entitled to it. Let me again emphasize that God does not forbid us enjoying all that he has given us. However, we may not cross the line into greed and self-indulgence. How is this to be achieved? The simple answer is, *through generosity*. Whenever you increase your income or make some extra money, immediately think of how you can *give away some or even all of it*. This is a simple principle: counter *greed* with *generosity*. Listen once again to Paul: "As for the rich in this present age … They are to do good, to be rich in good works, *to be generous* and ready to share, thus storing up treasure for themselves as a good foundation for the future" (1 Tim. 6:17–19). The money you give away does not always need to go directly to the Lord's work; it could simply be shared with someone who has less than yourself. Have you noticed that one statement Jesus made is not found in the Gospels but only in Acts, where it stands out all on its own? "In all things I have shown you that by working hard in this way we must help the weak and remember the words of the Lord Jesus, how he himself said, 'It is more blessed to give than to receive'" (Acts 20:35).

Treasure

The Bible teaches that "where your treasure is, there your heart will be also" (Matt. 6:21). One of the problems with all our possessions and our money is that we "treasure" them. They become important to us. We get upset when something is damaged, stolen or lost. How do you react if someone bashes your brand-new car the day you bought it? Or drops your vintage bone china on the floor? Or your camera? Most of us have endured experiences like this, and, if we are honest, we have shown where our hearts really are! We are not to treasure any of our possessions. Treasuring them is, like greed, a form of idolatry. We are to worship only one God. (I am not suggesting that we become reckless with our possessions; this would be poor stewardship.)

Confidence or trust

We should take seriously these further words of Jesus: "Do not lay up for yourselves treasures on earth, where moth and rust destroy and where thieves break in and steal, but lay up for yourselves treasures in heaven, where neither moth nor rust destroys and where thieves do not break in and steal" (Matt. 6:19–20). In the banking crisis of 2007–2009, my wife and I became very aware of the insecurity of our bank balances. We had invested, as we thought, in an ultra-conservative manner by putting our money into eight banks in four countries, avoiding any high-risk stock-market-linked investments. Then those very banks teetered! God spoke to us through that period and we changed our priorities, investing substantial sums in the Lord's work, where "neither moth nor rust destroys and where thieves do not break in and steal." The thieves in this crisis were all those who had gone beyond normal banking processes in their pursuit of greed. Let me emphasize again that, just because we trust God, we are not to be reckless in our investments. As good stewards we *must* make every effort to act responsibly. Our judgments may, however, fail us, and in the end we may have to accept failure. We are then forced to recognize that our real security truly lies in God's provision. If his hand is not in our actions, then they are futile anyway. God's hand is never in our sins, and misplaced trust is a sin.

Lessons from Proverbs

The book of Proverbs is often seen as a set of clever sayings which make good reading in a promise box or Chinese cookie. They are nothing of the sort, however, and should rather be seen as instructions that we should follow as we seek to live as God wants us to live. Throughout this book I quote often from Proverbs, but here are some of the many verses which deal specifically with our finances:

Honor the LORD with your wealth
    and with the firstfruits of all your produce;
then your barns will be filled with plenty,
    and your vats will be bursting with wine.   (3:9–10)

Blessed is the one who finds wisdom,
    and the one who gets understanding,
for the gain from her is better than gain from silver
    and her profit better than gold.
She is more precious than jewels,
    and nothing you desire can compare with her.   (3:13–15)

… riches do not last forever …   (27:24)

Giving to the Lord's work

I originally planned to write an entire chapter on this subject, but in the interests of brevity I will limit myself to just a few key points. I have dealt extensively with the subject in two other books,[3] and I could do it no better than Randy Alcorn in his excellent little book *The Treasure Principle*,[4] which I strongly recommend.

Let me simply summarize the ten principles of giving as outlined by J. Ligon Duncan in his booklet *Ten Principles for Christian Giving*:[5]

The Lord Jesus:
1. expects and requires us to give;
2. wants us to give for the right reasons;
3. wants us to practice benevolent or charitable giving;
4. reminds us that our giving is ultimately to the all-seeing heavenly Father.

And the Bible teaches that:
5. Christian giving is an act of worship;
6. Christian giving should be given in the light of the incarnation (i.e. sacrificially, as Jesus gave himself);

7. Christian giving should be done in accordance with our means;
8. the liberality of God's blessings to us is connected to the liberality of our Christian giving;
9. Christian giving must be willing giving, free giving;
10. Christian giving ought to be cheerful giving.

I would encourage you to read the booklet for more details and for the biblical proof for these principles.

In the following chapters I assume the biblical principles I have set out here. As you read, please therefore keep these principles in mind, and seek to make all your financial decisions as a good steward, avoiding greed, giving generously and not treasuring—nor placing your trust in—riches.

Notes

1 **John Temple,** *Be Successful, Be Spiritual: How to Serve God in the Workplace* (Leominster: Day One, 2008).

2 **Brian Rosner,** *Beyond Greed* (Kingsford, NSW: Matthias Media, 2006).

3 *Be Successful, Be Spiritual*; and *Make Your Church's Money Work: Achieving Financial Integrity in Your Congregation* (Leominster: Day One, 2008).

4 **Randy Alcorn,** *The Treasure Principle: Unlocking the Secret of Joyful Giving* (Sisters, OR: Multnomah, 2001).

5 **J. Ligon Duncan III,** *Ten Principles for Christian Giving* (Jackson, MS: First Presbyterian Church, n.d.).

Living within your means

I recall a lecturer at the business school I attended asking how many of us had a precise idea of what our families spent each month. One attendee was brave enough to raise his hand, surprising all of us, not least the lecturer. When asked how he knew, his reply was simple: "I know precisely what I earn and we spend 10 percent more than that each month." Sadly, this is probably true of many people, except that the excess spending may be even more than 10 percent. The gap between income and expenditure creates debt.

The first key to successful family finances is to live within your income and *not within your credit limit*.

Why do many of us fail in doing what is so obvious? As explained earlier, it is because of our desire to have more and consume more, *now*. We are not content with what we have. As James put it, "each person is tempted when he is lured and enticed by his own desire" (James 1:14); and, "You ask and do not receive, because you ask wrongly, to spend it on your passions" (4:3). This is a spiritual problem, and in particular a *worship* problem. It is idolatry. Any reader of the Old Testament will be disappointed by the number of times it tells us that the Israelites ceased to worship the God who had brought them out of slavery and instead served the gods of the people around them, yet we do precisely the same thing. We worship the *things around us* in place of God. We respond to the marketers and the advertisers. Make no mistake, we are bombarded from all sides with the message that we should consume and enjoy. The marketers are professionals and know how to entice us. How do we avoid succumbing?

As with all temptation, we cannot easily change our behavior. Most people will simply fail. We need the power of God's Spirit working within us, but we are also called upon to be proactive in avoiding the temptations. Look carefully at what Paul taught the Philippians: "Therefore, my beloved, as you have always *obeyed* ... *work out* your own salvation with fear and trembling, for it is *God who works* in you ..." (Phil. 2:12–13). Consider some of the actions (the "working out" bit) that *we* need to take to resist the temptations of living in our high-pressure world of advertising and consumerism:

- Do not read the glossy "good-life" magazines. These are filled with temptations to buy or consume what may not be remotely necessary. I have stopped even opening the airline magazines, which depict a way of life which is presented as normal but is not even close.
- Do not watch the "lifestyle" TV programs that extol glamorous or extravagant living.
- Hit the mute button when the commercials appear on TV and try to ignore what they are showing.
- Avoid impulse buying. When you go shopping, draw up a list of what you need to buy and wear blinkers for everything else. Never buy anything from the displays at the checkouts. (My wife came up with this one. I *am* trying!)
- Don't buy anything that is a bargain if you do not need it. It is no bargain if you can do without it.
- Politely decline any salesperson who comes to your door. He or she is almost always selling something that you do not need.
- Do not be tempted to have the latest in anything. This includes fashions, electronic gadgets, computers and cars. The list is endless. Keep your old one until it makes economic sense to replace it. I still wear suits that are twenty years old. They have been in and out of fashion a few times, so I am not always out of date! While ladies may be more tempted in the clothing arena, men will be subject to more pressure with gadgets and cars. Watch yourself.
- Do not spend ostentatiously. I recall a pastor's wife noting that many people who have money often live frugal lives and shop carefully, whereas some people tend to spend freely even if they should be more careful. The writer of Proverbs knew this long ago! "One pretends to be rich, yet has nothing; another pretends to be poor, yet has great wealth" (Prov. 13:7).

Women tend to control daily needs such as food and children's clothing. I have noticed that they are generally very good at saving on these items. However, I have also noticed that men are very good at spending all their wives' hard-fought savings! An entire year's discounts, grocery coupons and special offers go on a single new digital camera, mobile phone, TV set or computer. Men ought to be examples to their families, leading in frugality and not succumbing to the temptations of the materialistic market. Again, I am not saying that we cannot enjoy all that God has given us to enjoy; I am asking that fathers take a lead in setting good and appropriate priorities for expenditure.

Am I against advertising? Is it the advertisers' fault that we fail so badly in these areas? (I do, at least!) Not at all. Advertising fulfills a useful role in informing us of our choices and is a necessary element (maybe a necessary evil) in a free-market society. The problem lies with us. We are always to act responsibly and to resist temptation. How do we do this? The first step in winning this battle against our desires is by reading and obeying the Bible. We can only obey it if we read it regularly. The next step is to be a doer: "But be doers of the word, and not hearers only" (James 1:22). Then, most importantly, pray. Pray specifically about the temptations around you and ask God to do what his Word says he will do: "it is *God who works* in you ..." (Phil. 2:13). Pray with your spouse, pray with your family. When my youngest son used to accompany my wife to the supermarket, he would put items back on the shelf if they were not on the shopping list or within the family budget. *Get your family involved.*

What if you simply cannot make your income cover your expenditures, even though you have cut out everything that is not necessary to survive? Throughout the world there are over one billion people living at or below the "poverty line" for whom such a scenario is undoubtedly true. I have encountered such families even in the "rich" first or second worlds. To be in such a situation implies that you cannot reduce your spending any more. What should you do? Firstly, do not borrow apart from what may be needed to feed your family *in the short term.* You need to find a better-paying job. Write up a good "résumé" or CV and get this to every employment agency you can find, answer every advertisement and pray hard. If you have roughly thirty years of employment left, you will work a further 60,000 hours. Even if you only get $1 per hour more than in your previous job, that will add up to $60,000 over the rest of your working life. If you do not do this, you could find yourself in debt by that amount (or more) at the end of your working life.

Income

In the Bible, four legitimate sources of income are mentioned: earnings, inheritance, return on investment and gifts.[1] In this section I will mainly deal with earnings because this flows from "work," which is the basis of a biblical economy. It is probably the largest source of income for most of us during our working lives. The same principles apply to income sourced from a pension or from savings.

Many people choose a career driven by the earnings capability of that career. This is not in itself wrong and, indeed, I was encouraged at the beginning of my career to use my gifts to make money so that I could give as much money as I could to the Lord's work. Good stewardship surely supports this approach. But all too often our motive is solely to become wealthy and to create a "good life" for ourselves—in other words, to practice greed. As we have seen, enjoying all the things that God has provided for us is not in itself wrong. But our *motives* and the *use* to which we put our incomes are the big issues. We must answer the questions: Why should we earn as much as we can? How do we *spend* our incomes? What are our *attitudes* to our incomes and wealth? We have already looked at some of these issues but we need to expand them specifically as they relate to generating income.

Good stewardship calls on us to earn as much as we can within the bounds of our talents. Jesus taught that some of us get five talents, others two and some only one. In this parable, the two who used their talents well were both commended, but the one who did not use his talent at all was reprimanded, even cast out (Matt. 25:14–30). The next issue is what to do with our incomes. If you have a family, then the Bible is clear that you are to provide for them. "But if anyone does not provide for his relatives, and especially for members of his household, he has denied the faith and is worse than an unbeliever" (1 Tim. 5:8). Note that we are called upon first to provide for our own "household" and then for our relatives. In New Testament times, and in many cultures today, the household would have been an extended family. Precedents in the early church give us examples of caring for our Christian brethren, both in our own churches, in the wider church and finally for all people in the world. There are many passages from which we could prove these points but the following are sufficient:

As for the rich in this present age … They are to do good, to be rich in good works, to be generous and ready to share, thus storing up treasure for themselves as a good foundation for the future.   (1 Tim. 6:17–19)

Let the thief no longer steal, but rather let him labor, doing honest work with his own hands, so that he may have something to share with *anyone* in need.   (Eph. 4:28)

Next we need to consider our attitudes to income and how we should spend it. There are many best-selling books that set out the secret to becoming rich. Most propose a simple formula: earn as much as you can, live frugally, avoid waste, avoid debt and save as hard as you can. This is all good advice but it lacks one ingredient. *Why* do all this? It may be for very legitimate reasons, such as providing for our families or our old age. All too often, however, it is to indulge ourselves later. To do that is better than to "enjoy now and pay later," but it is nevertheless still within the credo of our society to "consume and enjoy." Greed becomes our consuming passion. As Christians we may enjoy what God has given us, but our passion should be to build God's work here on earth and to do good works with our wealth (look back at 1 Tim. 6:17–19 above). Riches must never become "treasure." Hoarding riches may simply be in order to boast or, perhaps with slightly more justification, to give us some sense of security. This is a fine point because we *are* required to be responsible stewards and to provide for ourselves and our families. The key issue is the extent of our hoarding and our attitude toward it. If we *treasure* these riches, or *trust* more in our riches than in our God, we have crossed the line.

The key lesson for succeeding with your family finances is to exercise *self-control* so that you live within your income. To do this you will have to look very carefully at your budget and perhaps reconsider your expenditure priorities.

Tax

You may be surprised that I include a section on this subject. The reason, however, is simple: tax may be your largest single item of expenditure!

Most of us probably dislike paying any tax at all (I am one such!). However, on this very subject Jesus taught us to "render to Caesar the things that are Caesar's, and to God the things that are God's" (Matt. 22:21). Paul reasoned that the government had a duty to protect its citizens and therefore argued, "For because of this you also pay taxes, for the authorities are ministers of God, attending to this very thing. Pay to all what is owed to them: taxes to whom taxes are owed …" (Rom. 13:6–7). When we resent paying taxes to wasteful or even corrupt governments (as I do!), we should remember that Jesus and Paul were writing about the Roman Empire.

Most Christians will, I hope, at least *intend* to be scrupulously honest in paying exactly what they are due to pay. Aim to join David in saying, "Vindicate me, O LORD, for I have walked in my integrity, and I have trusted in the LORD without wavering" (Ps. 26:1). On the other hand, I can see no reason at all why any of us should pay more than the law requires. That would be poor stewardship. Yet I suspect that many well-meaning Christians unknowingly infringe the law and probably also overpay, simply because they are not fully conversant with all that can be claimed. It is better to get both actions correct.

It is not possible to give a full analysis of all the tax laws that may affect individuals. Laws differ among countries and also change constantly. So instead I will give a few examples of tax issues which will hopefully alert you to ask the right questions of a local expert. Even if you pay only a little tax, I would advise you to get assistance, perhaps just by calling your local tax office. I have found these offices very helpful and it could save you some money or, worse, real embarrassment if you are caught inadvertently cheating on your tax! In the examples that follow, I highlight only some of the lesser-known issues which could cause you real problems.

1. GIFTS TO MISSIONARIES

A couple ask for financial contributions to enable them to do mission work in a foreign country. Someone gives them a large sum as a gift to help them on their way. Are there tax implications? In some countries, yes. As this is a person-to-person gift the person *making* the gift may be liable for "gift tax" or "donations tax." This could be anything from 20 to 40 percent of the amount. It is best to check with a local expert before making such a gift. What should the donor do if the gift does attract gift tax? Give the money to the mission society or the church and mark it as being for onward payment to the couple. In the USA, such a gift can be *deducted* from the donor's gross income, thereby *reducing* his or her tax bill. In the UK, this may also qualify for "gift aid," in which Inland Revenue will *add* some 25 percent to the gift (see under example 6 below). In South Africa, donations tax will be *payable* on everything above a threshold unless the gift is made to a suitably registered church or mission. In most countries, if the couple receive the money from a mission organization, they may have to pay income tax because the amount will be seen as a "salary." But this tax will almost certainly be less than the gift tax. This is a complicated situation because the next question concerns the country in which the tax will be levied. If the funds are received in the couple's home country, the tax laws of that country will apply. But if the money is received in the country where they work, its tax laws will also apply. I know missionaries who received funds over many years from outside their country of service and were then presented with huge tax bills once the authorities of that country caught up with them.

2. PAYMENT TO A FRIEND

You come to respect and love a friend who helps you by doing gardening, minding your dog and cleaning your car. One day you decide to give him or her a monetary gift. Is this taxable in your friend's hands, is it subject to gift tax or is it simply a gift? Again, the situation will differ from one country to another but generally it will depend on how much it is and *what you call it.* Please note that tax is often affected by what you say about it (i.e. the "form") as much as the "substance." Assume that the amount is large and therefore above the threshold that attracts "gift" or "donations" tax. If you simply give the money with a card that says something like "gift out of love and respect," the only possible tax then will be donations tax payable by you, the *giver.* But if you enclose a card that says something like, "in recognition for all your services," it will then be construed as payment and will be subject to income tax in the hands of the recipient, but not gift tax by you. Note that the substance is the same in both cases but your card can make the tax treatment very different!

I can think of only one exception to the gift tax rules. In some countries, spouses can give each other unlimited gifts that do not attract gift tax. However, there are some wrinkles. In South Africa, if the authorities think that the intention of the gift was to spread an investment over the couple in order to lower the tax rate on the interest earned, they can tax the interest at the highest rate of the couple. But this is not the case in the UK. It is worthwhile checking in the country where you are taxed.

3. GIFT OR DONATIONS TAX

This brings us to the next point: your motives or intentions. If the purpose of the gift to your kind friend above was *intended* as payment for services rendered, then it is taxable in your friend's hands as income regardless of what you say about it on your card. So, before you do anything, make sure that your intentions are clear. Remember that God judges our motives, so this is a tough one.

There are limitations on what you can simply give away without some tax liability. Some form of tax is generally payable in the hands of the *donor* once the aggregate of all donations exceeds a threshold which is different for each country. In South Africa, this includes the collection on Sundays unless the church has registered itself properly! UK taxpayers must also be careful about making donations to others, even to their children and grandchildren, because some donations are added back onto the donor's estate should he or she die within seven years of making the gift, and they may then be taxed at a high rate. The limit on these donations is generally quite low and covers everything from wedding presents to birthday presents. Beware!

In many cases you can *intend* to reduce your taxes by doing something entirely legal. Here is an example: you may put a large sum into someone's hands, quite legally, in such a way as not to attract gift or income tax in most countries by making the recipient an interest-free loan. This loan can then be "forgiven" by the amount that *is* allowed for gifts each year without tax consequences. But there are some wrinkles. As the loan is interest-free, the lost interest is itself deemed to be a gift and so must be included in any calculation of gift tax payable. Make sure that these amounts all tie up. You must bear in mind that you may die with some or all of the amount still owing to you. This amount should then return to your estate, where it may or may not attract death taxes (inheritance tax) depending on the size of your estate. It is, moreover, a good idea to leave the outstanding amount in your will to the recipient of the loan.

4. ODD-JOBBING

A man with good DIY skills accepts requests from his friends and acquaintances to do household repairs. They pay him in cash for his work. Being an honest man, he scrupulously maintains records of all this income and declares it as taxable income. However, he makes no deductions from this income, which means that he is *overpaying* tax. Here are some very legitimate costs which he could have deducted from his income:

- travel expenses associated with his services;
- possibly a tool allowance;
- part of his telephone account, especially any calls made that were specifically related to this enterprise, plus a pro rata portion of the line rental;
- if this enterprise becomes substantial, then a portion of the *interest* on any mortgage, if part of his house or workshop is used to store materials and tools;
- possibly some of the depreciation on his computer and other office equipment if he uses them to do his accounts or to source materials etc.

In a nutshell, all costs legitimately incurred in *generating income* may be deducted from income. In most countries, the man would not be required to register a company to enjoy these deductions.

5. CHILDREN'S TAX

In most countries, parents are responsible for their children's income. Sometimes this calls for inclusion of the child's income in that of the parents, and in other cases (e.g. in the USA), the child may be able to submit his or her own return ("kiddy" tax), which should reduce the tax payable.

6. CHARITABLE GIVING

You can increase your contributions to the Lord's work in the USA, Australia and the UK (and possibly in other countries as well) through careful tax planning. In the USA and Australia, you can deduct all contributions to approved charities and churches (in Australia, "deductible gift recipients") from your gross income. This reduces the tax you pay. It is good practice to increase your donation by the amount that you save by this method. If you do not know how to do the calculation, get your advisor to do it for you. In the UK, you can obtain the same result through "gift aid." This is a scheme in which for every £1 that you donate to a "charity" (including churches, missionary societies, etc.) the government will contribute a further 25p (at least) and you may still get an additional reduction on *your* tax bill. Some Christians are reluctant to use these means of increasing their giving, arguing that they do not want the state to contribute to the Lord's work. Surely this is faulty reasoning? The tax that is returned or saved is *your* money simply being returned. The same effect can be obtained in South Africa if the donations go to registered Bible colleges (and some other charities), while some tax relief may be available in other countries. It is worth checking with your tax advisor.

As mentioned above, I cannot give details for all the countries where this book may be read, and the information provided here is accurate only at the time of writing. I strongly recommend that you either consult an advisor or check for yourself by using the advisory bodies given in the endnotes.[2]

Notes

1 See Chapter 1 in *Be Successful, Be Spiritual.*
2 In the USA look under "Taxes" at: crown.org/library (there are many articles on tax here). In the UK consult "Money, Tax and Benefits" at: direct.gov.uk/en; or visit: taxcafe.co.uk. In Australia consult "Tax Deductible Donations" at: ato.gov.au/nonprofit/content.asp?doc=/content/66281.htm.

Debt

We have already seen that our culture encourages us to "consume and enjoy *now*"—often leading to debt. There is no biblical support for this approach, neither does it make sound economic sense.

Is all debt therefore wrong? The Bible does not say so, and the very fact that it limits both interest and terms indicates that debts will arise in a real, fallen world. However, God made this promise to his people:

And if you faithfully obey the voice of the LORD your God, being careful to do all his commandments that I command you today, the LORD your God will set you high above all the nations of the earth … The LORD will open to you his good treasury, the heavens, to give the rain to your land in its season and to bless all the work of your hands. And you shall lend to many nations, but you shall not borrow. (Deut. 28:1, 12)

This promise is given to the *nation of Israel* but surely it suggests two general principles: firstly, observing God's laws leads to prosperity; and, secondly, being a "borrower" is not God's best for any "Israelite," whether of the Old or New Testament variety (see also Prov. 22:7).

Some justifiable exceptions are also in order. In my book *Make Your Church's Money Work*, I proposed lending the pastor money to enable him to buy his own house or car. The spiritual issue is that this will enable him to be a better steward, rather than merely satisfy his desire for instant gratification.

Consider the following biblical instructions concerning debts:

- "You shall not charge interest on loans to your brother, interest on money, interest on food, interest on anything that is lent for interest. You may charge a foreigner interest, but you may not charge your brother interest, that the LORD your God may bless you in all that you undertake in the land that you are entering to take possession of it" (Deut. 23:19–20). I believe that this applies to the New Testament "Israelites," namely Christians today.
- Debts were to be forgiven every seven years (Deut. 15:1–11). This

means that if you do lend (or borrow) money, you had better make the term reasonably short!

- "When you make your neighbor a loan of any sort, you shall not go into his house to collect his pledge. You shall stand outside, and the man to whom you make the loan shall bring the pledge out to you. And if he is a poor man, you shall not sleep in his pledge. You shall restore to him the pledge as the sun sets, that he may sleep in his cloak and bless you. And it shall be righteousness for you before the LORD your God" (Deut. 24:10–13). In essence this teaches that the lender must respect the borrower's dignity (that he or she is made in God's image), and the borrower's need of warmth and comfort must not be taken from him or her through the surety that the lender offers.

- It is a sin to borrow and not repay. "The wicked borrows but does not pay back, but the righteous is generous and gives" (Ps. 37:21); "It is better that you should not vow than that you should vow and not pay" (Eccles. 5:5). If you borrow, you must not expect what you have borrowed to become a gift. However, the lender should be prepared not to get the loan back and should not ask for interest. Naturally, the borrower may well offer interest and should make every effort to repay. Nor may the lender sue his or her fellow believer in a secular court. Hear Paul: "When one of you has a grievance against another, does he dare go to law before the unrighteous instead of the saints?" (1 Cor. 6:1). We are told that it is better to be defrauded than to lose our witness by suing one another (1 Cor. 6:7). In Luke 6:30–31, the Lord said, "Give to everyone who begs from you, and from one who takes away your goods do not demand them back. And as you wish that others would do to you, do so to them." This is a clear statement of the principle of "fair exchange," which asks what you would do if the tables were turned. It does not absolutely state that a Christian should never sue to collect a debt *from a non-Christian*, but it does imply a higher standard of behavior from the Christian.

- Do not stand surety for a loan between two other parties. Note these verses from Proverbs: "Whoever puts up security for a stranger will surely suffer harm, but he who hates striking hands in pledge is secure" (11:15); "One who lacks sense gives a pledge and puts up security in the presence of his neighbor" (17:18); "Be not one of those who give pledges, who put up security for debts" (22:26).

- Jesus seemed to approve of a bank paying interest on investments. While the central message of the parable of the stewards was neither about profit nor interest, Jesus would hardly have used such an example if either practice were wrong. "Then you ought to have invested my money with the bankers, and at my coming I should have received what was my own with interest" (Matt. 25:27). This principle alone permits debt because the investing bank would have had to lend the money to someone else at interest.

Perhaps it would be a lot easier if God's Word did prohibit or even limit a Christian from borrowing, but it does not. We are therefore left to reason indirectly from other biblical principles as to how much debt is acceptable for a Christian.

Classes of expenditure

Before we proceed to discuss the practical implications of debt, I will divide all items of expenditure into just two classes: consumption expenditure and investment expenditure.

"Consumption expenditure" includes those items which lose their value once you have used them or completed the service. A good example is food. You buy it and eat it. It is then gone forever. The same is true of most entertainment, travel, holidays or even clothing. Even expenditure on medicine or health care is consumption. Once you have paid for it, it is unlikely that you will ever get your money back again. However, if you have spent wisely, these services should do you good. You receive the benefits of the expenditure in maintaining your life, curing your illness or improving your education. Even entertainment has a value. While you should have no problem paying for these items, you must nevertheless be very frugal, as you never get your money back.

On the other hand, "investment expenditure" becomes an "asset" which remains yours. If you so desired, you could sell the item and get some of your money back. Sometimes a "service" becomes an investment; for example, hiring a builder (a service trade) to build you a house will result in you owning an asset. Education improves your ability to earn and can also be seen as an asset.

There are two kinds of assets: those that appreciate (gain value in time) and those that depreciate (lose value in time). A good example of the first is a good property; of the second, a car. There may be any number of other assets which may go either way, such as a painting, carpet or piece of furniture. Sometimes an item may appear to be an asset but may depreciate so fast that it becomes a consumption item. A good example is everyday furniture, which quickly loses value. Another is clothing. Sometimes a purchase may superficially be an asset but it is so poorly chosen that you can never recover its value. It then becomes a consumption item. This can be true of a badly chosen property or renovations to a perfectly sound property. If renovations do not enhance the resale value of the property by at least what they cost, they are not an asset at all. Much care must be exercised in how you spend money in any of these gray areas.

In making judgments about spending or investing money, you must determine which type of expenditure you are considering. Obviously, investments are a good way of using your money while consumption spending is gone forever and should be very carefully considered.

Loans

If we accept that we are stewards of all that we have, or desire to have, then every time we borrow we have to ask whether or not it is good stewardship. In general, I suggest that the following are poor acts of stewardship.

- Any loan for consumption expenditure. I would almost argue that such loans should never happen. However, there are exceptions. You may have fallen on very hard times and are forced to borrow simply to feed your family. It would be breaking the even higher principle of neglecting your family if you refused a loan under these circumstances. There may be other serious situations, such as illness or any other disaster. But none of these is the norm.
- Any loan for the following: an overseas vacation, a party (even a wedding), clothing, entertainment, sport or any luxury item such as jewelry, watches, cameras or expensive clothing—in short, any *nonessential* consumption.

- Any debt which cannot reasonably be repaid. The Bible is clear on this (see above), yet many people, including Christians, run up impossible debts on their credit cards or overdrafts.
- Any debt where the value of the product is less than the realizable value of the asset. A good example is buying a house using a mortgage that is larger than the resale value of the property. It also often happens with purchases such as cars where no deposit is required; since cars depreciate very rapidly, the debt will exceed the value of the car (this is often referred to as "negative equity" or being "under water"). This is dealt with more fully below.
- Any debt obtained at high interest rates. Many credit cards (especially store cards) charge from 15 to 30 percent p.a. and then charge all manner of additional fees which are set out in the fine print. This is poor stewardship.

What debts are legitimate? I suggest that you should try to avoid debt altogether, and, if you are already in debt, try your best to get out of it. However, I realize that this may not be practical, so here are a few general guidelines.

- Any debt which is incurred for a capital item and where the value of the item always exceeds the value of the debt can be seen as no debt at all since the loan is simply set off against the value of the item. The difference between the asset and the loan is your "equity" (i.e. what you actually own). A mortgage of, say, 80 percent of the value of a sound house is a good example.
- A debt which will increase your earning power in the future is legitimate. Study loans are good examples. These are often at low interest rates. But you must then complete the course and *use the knowledge* gained. Another example is equipment which enables you to accomplish more, such as an electric saw if you are a carpenter.
- All debt must be at reasonable interest rates and terms of repayment. A popular technique is to consolidate all your debt into one large debt and then focus on repaying it. This is a good way of seeing the magnitude of the problem and simplifying the administration. But check on the interest rate. If it is higher than the average that you are already paying, it is not a good idea.

- If there is such a thing as a "good" debt, it is a modest bank overdraft. The great advantage of an overdraft is that you may be charged a reasonably low interest rate and any spare cash you may have, or any delays in cashing outgoing checks, will reduce the overdraft and hence the interest paid.
- As stated above, never, ever use your credit card to accumulate debt. The interest rates are horrific and the temptation to run up these debts is very high.
- Finally, remember that it is *futile to save and borrow at the same time.* Use your savings to clear your debts. If you don't, you are borrowing at a high interest rate (say 6 percent or higher) and saving at a lower rate (say 4 percent or lower). You are, in effect, borrowing your own money back and enriching the banks by at least 2 percent in the process! I know you may ask about the "rainy day" when you suddenly need cash. Others will insist that it is good to save. Yes, it is good to save, but the *best way to save is by repaying your own debts.* This also has tax advantages. Most savings pay interest which is taxable, whereas in most countries (except the USA for a house mortgage) the interest on your debts gets you no tax relief. So the value of interest *income* is diminished by tax, widening the real gap between *what you pay to the bank* and *what the bank pays to you.* Pause here for a moment. If the best way to save is to clear your debts, then even better is not to get into debt in the first place. Most people will argue that they have no option for capital items such as a house or a car. Probably this is true for the house, and in any event houses tend to appreciate, so owning one is generally a good idea, even with a mortgage. Think carefully, however, before getting into debt for a car. You will pay a very high interest rate and own a depreciating asset (see Chapter 7).

If you plan to save and cannot get by without a mortgage, try to use one of the mortgages which allow you to repay a variable amount each month and to withdraw any overpayment with ease. In South Africa, these are called "access bonds"; in the UK, "offset mortgages," "plus bonds" or "draw down mortgages." In the USA, nearly the same effect can be achieved by using a "home equity loan" linked to a mortgage. By using one of these mortgages you can pay off your mortgage at a higher rate than is necessary but you can easily withdraw cash from the mortgage if you run into the proverbial rainy day and have to withdraw from your savings. You therefore do not need to create a separate savings account. Incidentally, your bank will not be keen on you following this advice because, as illustrated above, it will lose interest income.

Your home

S hould you buy or rent your home? On purely economic grounds the answer is not clear cut. A simple analysis suggests that renting means that over many years you are paying out a lot of money for which you get nothing permanent in its place. You have made your housing costs part of "consumption" spending, whereas it seems more sensible to make it part of your "investment" expenditure. However, on a closer look you will discover that, if you bought your house using a mortgage, then interest, similar in value to the rent, will be paid to the bank and is also lost. In addition, when you own the property you have to take on all the risks of ownership and all the "consumption" spending such as maintenance, property taxes, insurance and so on. Nevertheless, I am a firm believer in every family purchasing its own home for these reasons:

- It *is* a fine method of saving. Most of us do not have the discipline to rent a house and then invest whatever saving we might make each month. Your mortgage forces you to do so.
- It gives a sense of permanence. Families do well if they live consistent and predictable lives. The temptation to change jobs, cities or even countries is tempered by the drastic measures that are called for in changing houses. I am not suggesting that you should not move house. It may be necessary for good reasons, such as a growing family or even a career move. I am merely saying that fickle moves will be restrained.
- Provided that you keep up the mortgage payments (or get ahead) you are secure and cannot be asked to move outside of your own control. For this reason you will devote more time and energy to maintaining the house and garden and creating what we call a "home." This is a good and valuable environment in which to raise a family and will result, in most cases, in an appreciating asset.
- Consider the ultimate result of saving over many years. You will own your own home free of debt. Your pension needs will be reduced. You may even decide to scale down and convert your larger and more valuable home into a smaller one, thereby releasing cash on which to live during your pension years ("down-sizing").

Apart from tax, the highest item on most families' budgets will be their homes. It should therefore enjoy the most scrupulous attention. Once again, it is impossible to give detailed advice about buying a property because it will be different for every country, even city, and for different needs. Nevertheless, there are certain general principles which apply to all property purchases. Naturally you should buy a property that meets the needs of your family, but, as this is such a major item, you should also make it a *sound investment*. What are the key issues?

Location

You will have heard many times that location is the single most important factor in determining the value of a property. It is. However, location in itself is a matter of perception and no consistent rules apply. You will have to do some research to discover the best locations for each category house in your target area. In theory, the property value should be enhanced by access to major roads and public transport, and proximity to shops, schools, hospitals and places of employment. Further enhancing attributes are view, general standards within the neighborhood and the extent to which the area looks green or "leafy." On the other hand, features like a railroad or a busy thoroughfare may reduce value. However, exceptions occur for inexplicable reasons, so do your homework. Scarcity value will also push up prices. This occurs along a coastline or wherever development is limited. This is not to say that everyone should clamor to buy a unique property in an expensive area; it may be beyond your budget. Equally sound investments may be made in average-priced locations where most of the needs of an average family are met. These are the so-called "John Citizen" locations. They make good investments because a large market always exists for such properties provided that they suffer no defects and are priced correctly.

However, a most important issue in location is proximity to a good church. It may even make your choice less attractive in other respects. Before even deciding on a general area, check out all the local churches and make sure that you can settle in at least one of them. Then draw a circle on a map with your chosen church at the center; the radius of the circle will be determined by the distance you deem practical to travel to the church.

Eliminate those sectors that are completely unsuitable and rank the remaining sectors according to the economic and convenience aspects listed above. Search in these sectors.

Curb appeal
Never buy a property that looks bad or out of place in the neighborhood even if it is a mansion inside. It will not sell well because most buyers will not stop long enough to look at it. Buy a home that looks like a typical home within the community where you intend buying.

Placing
The placing of the property on the site is also important. Generally, because of the sun, in the southern hemisphere the living areas should face north, and in the northern hemisphere they should face south. Also check where the property is placed on the site. In a typical British suburb this may be determined for you, but elsewhere you should check that the house leaves adequate parking in the front and enough outside space at the back to enjoy or in which to allow the children to play safely.

Value
Never buy the most expensive property in the neighborhood. Smart buyers who believe that location is more important than any other factor will compare this expensive house with one at the lower end of a more expensive neighborhood. This house will therefore have to compete not only with others in its own area, but also with houses in the next-priced area. Try to stay within the typical price range for a given sub-division or suburb. You should also negotiate on price. I was surprised when I discovered that in the UK, the advertised price is merely a guide and that houses often change hands at a higher price (they also often change hands at a much lower price; it depends on the demand for the property). In South Africa, where I did several hundred property deals, the rule is to pay *less*. In Australia, properties are sold through auction, while in the UK it is possible to "gazump" a buyer. This is a practice in which, until the contracts have been exchanged, it is possible for another buyer to offer a higher price and acquire the property. To a point, the English and

Australian systems reflect market conditions more fairly but they prolong finalizing the deal.

Design

You must determine what size house you need in order to accommodate your family, but it is also important that what you buy will sell again (remember that your home should be an appreciating asset). This means knowing what features are popular in the community where you intend living. You should also make sure that the house has no design flaws. For example, having one bedroom leading into another may work for you if you have, say, two sons, and one son does not mind the other son walking through his bedroom. If, however, the next buyer has a son and a daughter, this will be seen as a drawback which may prevent a sale.

It is also important to determine the features that are likely to be wanted in the future. Forty years ago, most families were content with a single bathroom, but my perception is that few families now will buy a house that does not offer at least one family bathroom and one en-suite. Other features that have become "standard" are a conservatory or a family room. This is all part of the rising standard of living that I referred to earlier. Is it extravagant to invest in these features? Yes, if you cannot afford them, but no, if you can. Why is this? Because your home is an "investment" and not "consumption" spending.

Technical review

In some countries it is mandatory to have certain checks done on various elements of a property. In South Africa, for example, a certified electrician must issue the seller with a certificate approving the electrical work, and an expert must certify that no wood beetles are in the roof timbers. In the UK, it is usual to get a surveyor to check the house over and the law demands a Home Information Pack (HIP) to be supplied by all sellers. Something similar is required in the USA but the survey can be coupled to insurance which covers the new owner should anything go wrong within a specified time. All these checks are good up to a point. You will, however, discover that the professionals who check your future house will always add a disclaimer in the fine print in which they accept no responsibility for their surveys. They are therefore of limited value. Underlying all this is the presumption that the "buyer is to beware." So you should take a good look yourself. Your attorney should also check carefully that the legal owner has the right to be selling and so on. In the USA, further pitfalls are possible. If the house has been worked on in the recent past, you have to determine that all the materials have been paid for. If not, the vendor may demand that you, as the beneficial user of the materials, either pay for them or give them back. You can end up paying twice! All countries have their wrinkles!

A few critical practical points:

- Try to avoid flat roofs and even "box gutters," because they are trying to defy gravity by stopping water from flowing to the ground.
- As the roof is a major item, have it well checked.
- Check the electrical wiring carefully. Electricity is a dangerous commodity and we tend to use it without considering how easily it can bring disaster into our homes. Ensure that the wiring is reasonably new, that the circuit-breakers are of a modern type (no wire fuses) and that, at the very least, all plug outlets have "earth leakage protection." These devices trip the circuit if a fault to earth is detected (which could be you touching a live wire) and are also sometimes named "residual current devices" (RCD or RCB) or "ground fault breakers" (GFB). They cost a few dollars and could save someone's life.
- In climates where air-conditioning or heating is a significant cost, look carefully, as a good steward of your money, at insulation. In most countries, natural gas will give you the lowest heating bill but modern "reverse cycle" air-conditioning systems are even cheaper despite their use of electricity.

Legal issues

Legal procedures differ substantially around the world and so here I simply highlight a few additional points to trigger buyers and sellers to ask questions. In practice, property transactions are concluded in writing and require at least one legal expert to handle the process. In England, the transaction can be very protracted and the buyer cannot gain entry to the property until a deposit (usually 10 percent) has been paid and contracts, signed by the seller and owner, have been exchanged. In the USA, Scotland and South Africa, an offer in writing can be signed by the parties (or by someone holding a special power of attorney, usually the seller's or buyer's attorneys) and this then becomes binding, even though it may be subject to any number of conditions. The deal can only fall through if one of the conditions fails. Familiarize yourself with the process *before you start out*, as it will cost a lot of money and you can be trapped in any number of ways. In the USA, the process is simple and can be very swift, as it is all done by attorneys operating in the private sector.

Mortgage

Much as I dislike debt, I think one exception is permissible, and that is a mortgage on your property. I allow this partly because the property is not really all yours until the mortgage has been repaid. You effectively buy it by degrees. The portion that you do own at any point in time is known as your "equity." A few words of caution. Firstly, never take out a mortgage which is higher in value than that of the property. As mentioned before, this gives rise to "negative equity," also referred to as being "under water," which is a good description because you will be drowning in debt! Some countries ban mortgages of more than about 75–80 percent of the value of the property, and I consider this to be prudent. Had such a policy been followed in all Western countries, our current debt crisis may never have occurred. In addition, monthly mortgage repayments should not be more than 25 percent of your reasonable, sustainable level of income. Young couples should be careful about using combined income, as the arrival of children may alter this amount.

It is wise to insure your mortgage; indeed, the mortgage provider may insist on it. Here is a money-saving tip: get quotes from several insurance companies before you take the insurance offered to you by the mortgage provider. Invariably these linked insurance policies are much more expensive than ones you can obtain yourself. You may have to stand your ground on this issue as the mortgage companies (or their salespeople) often earn high commissions on these policies.

The family car

Afte your home and possibly your tax, your car or cars form the largest item of expenditure in your budget and one which I, as a young man, was told would always keep me poor! The bad news is that it is mostly *consumption* expenditure. Even worse, it has the potential to drain your finances in unexpected ways. Yet most of us buy and sell our cars on emotion and never fully appreciate the cost elements. If you need to get out of debt and put your finances on a sound footing, *this is the place to start.*

Whenever I speak to people about the cost of their cars, they normally complain about the cost of fuel (gas [petrol] or diesel). But, frankly, that is one of the lesser problems. Let me give a rough breakdown of owning and operating a typical family car.

- Assume you own a small family car costing $12,000 when new.
- Assume that, after six years, you sell the car for $2,000 and that you depreciate it on a straight-line basis; the average annual capital loss is $1,666.
- Assuming you paid cash, the interest lost on the capital at just 5 percent p.a. is $600. (If you bought the car on credit, the interest will generally be much higher, averaging around $1,500.)
- If you drive about 10,000 miles p.a., fuel will cost about $1,000.
- Insurance for a year will cost about $300.
- Routine maintenance over a year will cost about $300.
- Road tax (or car tag) will cost about $100.
- This is all at the minimum, but it adds up to $3,966, or $4,866 if you bought your car on credit, per year.

What is noteworthy is that the largest amount, equal to 67 percent of the total, lies in the cost of merely owning the vehicle. If the car was bought on credit, the total will rise to 73 percent! These figures will reduce somewhat in the UK as gas (and diesel) is roughly twice the cost in the USA but distances traveled may be less. I recommend that everyone does this calculation accurately as different countries or states, as well as personal circumstances, will vary.

Consequently, if you want to save a significant amount of money on your car, *start with the initial outlay: buy a cheaper car.*

This means buying carefully. Deciding on the make, size and model of your car is very much a matter of personal needs and taste. You are always responsible for your own buying decisions *and the consequences of those decisions.* Remember that you are to be a good steward.

There are several different approaches to car ownership. One is to keep the car running but spend nothing on its appearance, and to drive it until it literally stops running, at which point you scrap it. This is sometimes known as the "wheelbarrow method" because that is how you treat your wheelbarrow. The other is to keep it in perfect condition in every way and to exchange it after a reasonable period and number of miles. I personally prefer the latter, but I can offer no definite proof that this approach is more economic than the former. In both cases you *must* save to replace it without incurring debt.

One thing, however, is very clear. In the twenty-first century, depreciation of a new car is anything but uniform over the lifetime of the car. Figures in 2009 suggest that new cars may depreciate by up to 40–50 percent in the first year, depending on the make and model. This means that if you buy the family car suggested in the example above when it is one year old, you will pay about $7,000 for it. Naturally, if you sell it after the six years suggested, you will get less for it as it will then be *seven* years old. Assuming that you get just $1,250 when you sell it, then over six years you will write off an average of $958 over the six years. The lost interest also drops to $350, and the total annual cost drops to $3,008. The ownership costs are down to $1,708, about 57 percent of the total annual expenditure. If you are on a tight budget, you can make no case for buying a new car, especially if you can buy a used one with low mileage and a good warranty from a reputable dealer and at a low price. Yet I notice that many young people, often directly from college or even school, make straight for the new-car showroom and buy a new car, *almost always on credit.* Buying a new car is not always wrong, but it may reflect poor judgment in regard to your priorities and also demonstrate that you have succumbed to the temptations mentioned in earlier chapters. Certainly, buying a new car on credit when you have just left college or school seems an unjustified choice of priorities. Rather, save all you can to invest (note: invest, not spend) in a property. Beware of the salesperson who is trained to sell to you on the basis of "affordability," meaning low monthly payments. He or she will seldom point out the huge interest bill which you will be paying in addition to the price of the car.

What if you do not have the cash to buy a car at all? The simple answer is, go without if at all possible. In the UK, it is entirely possible to avoid buying a car. I know several people who manage well using public transport or taxis all the time. I know one man (in his sixties) who has never even held a driver's license. This is different in the USA, South Africa, Australia and perhaps other places where this book may be read. But do consider the option. Only as a reluctant last resort should you buy the car on credit. Even then, you may be able to use some alternative means of borrowing. Speak to your bank manager about an overdraft. I have already explained the advantages of an overdraft (see Chapter 5): you will get a much better interest rate, and any spare cash you may have will reduce the overdraft and hence the interest paid.

When buying a car (whether new or used) from a dealer,

- beware of the wiles of the salespeople. Remember, they are professionals trained to sell to you. They will quickly pick up your fascination for a particular (often trivial) feature. As I said before, we tend to buy a car on emotion. It is all about our perception of ourselves driving it or our desire to show off.
- beware of the glossy sales brochures. Most cars are actually quite ordinary, and a day out of the showroom the car will *look* very ordinary.
- try to buy the cheapest car available that will do the job. Remember that at least 50 percent of the total cost of running the car is locked up in the purchase price. Avoid the added features and getting the "GL" instead of the "G" and so on (sometimes the difference lies in the stripe along the side!). Manufacturers offer "entry-level cars" which are utilitarian but adequate. They do not want to sell you one of these as they will make no money, or may even lose, if you buy one. They are so-called "loss leaders," aimed at getting you into the showroom and then "selling up" to increase their profit margins.

If you are forced to buy on a credit agreement (what used to be known as "hire purchase"), and have no alternative, bear these additional points in mind:

- Check the interest rate. Normally it will be about 15 percent p.a., but on occasions manufacturers will offer low-cost finance in order to move stock. They may simply add the interest to the purchase price, and you will discover that you could do better buying a competitor's car and paying a higher interest rate.

- Some manufacturers will offer you free finance for a period, allowing you to pay capital only over the period. It makes complete *economic* sense to take this provided that you put the unused cash into a savings account, earn interest on it and then pay the amounts each month from this account. But check the fine print. It will almost certainly include a clause which says that if you fail to pay just one of the monthly payments on time, the entire deal will revert to one *with interest* at some horrific rate. Some dealers go even further in trapping you, sending you an invoice each month to make sure that you remember to pay. Once you are lulled into a sense of security, they stop sending a reminder. You fail to pay and suddenly you are faced with a huge interest bill! You have been warned. Unless you can establish a very secure and automatic monthly payment, do not fall for one of these schemes.

- Check the fine print of what you agree to. The law can be quite draconian if you do not pay to the end. Even then, you may discover that you do not own the car and will have to pay for part of it again to take it over. Most credit agreements do not permit you to pay off the loan early unless you still pay *all the outstanding interest*. So whatever you do, read the fine print and then abide by what you have signed up for. Any changes, such as changing your car before the final payment or even trying to get out of debt, can be devastating. This is illustrated in the case study below.

Example: Financing cost

Imagine you buy a car on credit for $12,000 without a deposit—a situation to which I am totally opposed, as you will understand from the study.

- Payments spread over four years at 15 percent p.a. interest will be $330 per month.
- The total actually paid out is $15,832—i.e. the interest on this loan is a massive $3,832 or an average of $958 p.a.
- Now assume that after a year you decide to change the car for a newer one also costing $12,000 and that at this stage your original car has dropped in value to $9,000. (If you bought it new, the decline would be more.) How would the car dealer recalculate your payments?
- Firstly, he would calculate that you still owe thirty-six payments at $330 per month—i.e. $11,880.
- He would then deduct from this the part-exchange (or trade-in) value of your old car ($9,000), leaving you still indebted by $2,880 ($11,880-$9,000). This means that you have "negative equity" in the car, or are "under water" to this extent.
- The dealer would *add* this $2,880 to the cost of the new car (allowing no credit for the interest saved as a result of early payment)—i.e. calculate that you now owe $12,000 + $2,880 = $14,880.
- The monthly payments on this $14,880 will be $409 per month for a *new* period of forty-eight months.
- What have you gained? The same car, a year younger.
- What have you lost? A whole year of extra payments at the higher value of $409—i.e. $4,908 plus the higher monthly cost of $79 over the remaining three years. This all adds up to $7,752 *extra*! Your $12,000 car has actually cost you a massive $23,590, virtually double the face value! You thought you had achieved a fair trade-in (part-exchange) when in reality you were fooled. Does this horrify you? It should do. Yet I constantly hear of people pursuing this sort of practice and then complaining that they struggle financially. This situation is not unusual. I have known worse; for example, when a large "balloon" payment was also required at the end of the forty-eight months otherwise the car would revert to the dealer with no payment to the owner.

Remember that you are to be a good steward of all that falls under your control.

Leasing

Some car salespeople will encourage you to lease a car. This is especially true if you are a professional and have your car registered in your income-earning business. The sales pitch will point out the big advantage to you of the full lease payment being an allowable expense for tax purposes, saving you as much as 40 percent of the cost. This may well be true if the car is used solely in the generation of income, but what the dealer may not tell you is that leases are wonderful business for the banks and that the salesperson will receive a large "kickback" for selling you the lease. Furthermore, the dealer is not likely to point out that if you owned the car outright you would be permitted to deduct the depreciation on the car *and* the interest charges on any credit agreement. These two together will be close to the same amount as the lease charge—in other words, you end up very close to the same after-tax situation. In the case of outright ownership, the car will also be yours when paid for, whereas when leasing you will probably end up with nothing. If you pay cash, you will not only be able to claim the depreciation as a tax-deductible expense but you will save the interest and so be better off (see the case study above). In addition, you will save the tax on the interest earned on the cash that you had previously invested. In some countries, clever schemes do exist which make both the lease charge and the depreciation allowable tax expenses, but I am assuming that most readers are not driven by this sort of tax reduction. In general, avoid leasing.

Gas or diesel?

If you look at the calculations above you will note that the gas cost is actually a lesser consideration. If you have to pay a higher price for a diesel car, it is unlikely that you will recover the difference despite the undoubted increased economy of a diesel engine. Typically, a diesel engine will be 20–30 percent more economical than a petrol engine. In the example above, this would save you a maximum of $300 p.a.—not enough to justify more than about $1,000 in the cost of the vehicle. However, diesel engines tend to last longer so there may be other savings if you are planning to keep the car for a very long time.

Hybrid or electric?

I am all in favor of electric cars. My main reason is that they do not pollute the streets, they are efficient, and the electric motor is the ideal drive for all transportation. Most trains use electric traction for that reason. The electric car needs no gear-box or differential, a motor can be attached to each wheel creating perfect four-wheel drive, and the required torque or power can be closely matched to any situation. Costs will tumble once electric cars are in large-scale production. However, there is a problem. At present, batteries can only hold about half the energy that an equivalent-sized gas tank holds. This problem is rapidly being overcome (lithium ion batteries with ten times the current capacity are being demonstrated in the laboratory), and one day quite soon we may all be driving electric-powered cars. In the meantime, hybrids are one solution. These cars use gas engines which provide power alongside the electric motors and also charge the batteries as the car goes along. If you can get a hybrid at or near the same price as a gas or diesel car, buy it.

However, do not be misled. Carbon issues are not relevant unless a source of energy other than fossil fuels is used to generate the electricity used to power the car. Not polluting the streets is, however, a real advantage and is good stewardship of the earth

One or two cars?

It is common for families to own two cars and in many societies this is almost essential. The father uses one to go to work and the mother runs a taxi for the children. But is this really a necessity? Fathers should look at other means of getting to work. Use public transport, travel with a colleague or ride a bicycle. Maybe you could even walk. You must calculate whether or not the *assumption* is true that you need two cars. Look above at the cost of driving each car. When I was working away from home the accepted wisdom was for the father to own the large car and drive in it on his own to work. The mother had a small second car into which she crammed all the children. Looking back, I realize that I fell for this nonsense for several years. I mention this because we all too easily fall in line with what everyone else is doing (at least I did). Stop doing that. Think everything through as a good steward.

Family budget

The word "budget" may conjure up all sorts of resistance in your mind. You may see it as a financial exercise beyond your knowledge or capability. I plan to show that it is not and that it can be fun for the whole family. It is also biblical. Listen to Jesus's words: "For which of you, desiring to build a tower, does not *first sit down and count the cost*, whether he has enough to complete it?" (Luke 14:28). Jesus was not really speaking about building a tower but about counting the cost of following him, but would he have used this example if he expected the answer to be "none of us"? He went on to point out that a person who failed to plan or budget would be ridiculed. We turn again to Proverbs for wisdom: "The *plans* of the diligent lead surely to abundance, but everyone who is hasty comes only to poverty" (Prov. 21:5).

We saw in Chapter 3 that our clear motive for all we do must be to glorify God by obeying his commands. While this does not preclude enjoying all that God has given us, his commands have much more to do with providing for our needs and then sharing and giving. We therefore approach budgeting with this purpose in mind.

Who should budget? Perhaps you think that you are so poor that nothing short of a large injection of cash will help. Perhaps you are rich and are not concerned about money. Or perhaps everything is on an even keel and you think that you have no need for a budget. I have been in all of these situations and have found that a budget is essential in all cases. The most important lesson to be learned in budgeting is the *setting of priorities*. The budget is the tool that we use to make sound priority decisions. If you are struggling to get out of debt, the budget will highlight the size of the problem and show up areas that will simply have to be cut. If you are on an even keel or even well off, the budget will show how much is available to give away or save for your pension and so on.

Determine the starting point

The story is told of an Irishman who was approached by a lost motorist and was asked the way to Dublin. The Irishman stroked his beard and replied slowly, "Well, if I was setting out for Dublin I wouldn't start from here." Whenever we set out on a journey, we must start out from where we are. We need to know where that is. Proverbs endorses this:

Know well the condition of your flocks,
    and give attention to your herds …
the lambs will provide your clothing,
    and the goats the price of a field.
There will be enough goats' milk for your food,
    for the food of your household
    and maintenance for your girls.   (27:23, 26–27)

These verses appear to be speaking of farming assets, but how would the writer have phrased them today? Perhaps: "Know the state of your assets, your investments … they will provide income for your family."

So first determine your present "net worth" by assessing your assets. These are what you own (investments) less your liabilities (what you owe). Accountants call this making your personal "balance sheet" but do not let jargon put you off. This process is for everyone and is very simple. Make a list of all that you own, including those things that are mortgaged or financed on credit. Next, make a list of all that you owe under the heading "liabilities." You should value your assets at "fair market price," which is the price that you could reasonably sell them for. This has little to do with what you paid for them. That beautiful print that you purchased on impulse on your last vacation is probably worth nothing, so count it as nothing! To assist you in this exercise I have set out a list in Appendix 1 which you can convert to a spreadsheet. If you wish to go into it in more detail and are nervous about doing it on your own, you can download my MS Excel spreadsheets from the Day One Web site.[1]

This exercise may alarm you, because you may well find that your liabilities exceed your assets—in other words, that you are actually bankrupt! This may make you anxious, but listen to what Jesus had to say about this very practical issue: "Therefore do not be anxious, saying, 'What shall we eat?' or 'What shall we drink?' or 'What shall we wear?' For … your heavenly Father knows that you need them all" (Matt. 6:31–32).

Paul reinforced this: "do not be anxious about anything, but in everything by prayer and supplication with thanksgiving let your requests be made known to God" (Phil. 4:6). This may be the time for much prayer, starting *with repentance*, because you may well have spent unwisely and that may be the cause of your distress. Cheer up! God's grace extends to all our sins and misjudgments, provided that we confess them humbly to him.

If the above exercise does reveal that you are bankrupt, you must add an adequate amount into your spending budget which will eliminate this shortfall in a reasonable period, such as two or three years. This will translate into *reducing debt*. Clearly this will put pressure on your spending, but you simply must do it because you are in danger of being declared bankrupt. Take whatever action is needed to rectify the situation. I know of several friends who have sold their houses and moved into cheaper neighborhoods or smaller houses in order to clear their debts.

If, on the other hand, you discover that your net worth is substantial, you may reduce the amount of capital that you need for your pension and also the amount for which you need to insure yourself. This may free up more to give away.

Spending budget

Howard Dayton suggests that if the word "budget" frightens you, call this a spending "plan."[2] It does not matter what you call it, just make sure you do it! A strong word of advice: approach this subject prayerfully. Note the words quoted above: "... by prayer and supplication with thanksgiving let your requests be made known to God" (Phil. 4:6). Get the whole family praying.

I strongly recommend that you use an MS Excel spreadsheet such as I have included as a model budget in Appendix 2. You can set this up yourself, suitably modified for your family needs, or you can download my spreadsheets from the Day One Web site.[3]

You will note in my model that this list is separated into two types: those items that are "non-discretionary" and those items that are "discretionary." Determining the difference is a tough call because you will be surprised at the items you previously thought were "essential" and which are actually "discretionary." It is up to you and your family to decide on your priorities, always remembering that your decisions will have consequences. If you elect to spend heavily on vacations or entertainment when your children are young, it may damage your ability to provide for your old age. Perhaps you are content with this, but when you are older you may find that you struggle. We must each prayerfully determine our spending priorities. Look carefully at spending on items such as newspapers and magazines (you could instead use the Internet), movies and theater tickets (you could instead rent DVDs), sports matches (you could instead watch them on TV or the Internet), and at restaurants, coffee shops and so on. Buying one cup of coffee from a coffee shop every working day will cost you nearly $300 per year, which will go a long way toward paying your gasoline bill! Is this an "essential"? Do not forget your contribution to the Lord's work and to what you "share." Compare this amount with the items that constitute "entertainment."

One essential item in your budget is provision for your pension. This may be taken care of by your employer, but it should be checked for both security and adequacy. We will look at this in detail in Chapter 11.

Another essential item is saving for the "rainy day." As mentioned in Chapter 5, one good way to do this is to overpay any mortgage, so that you also effectively earn (actually save) the mortgage interest rate on these savings. All you have to ensure is that you can gain access to this overpayment when you need it. In South Africa, this is easily accomplished by using an "access bond" (or any of its equivalents), which is a mortgage that allows you to pay additional cash into your mortgage (thereby reducing your interest bill) but also to draw cash *out of* your mortgage at any time without any penalty. In the UK, various forms of "offset mortgages" give you the same privileges. In the USA, you can arrange a "home equity loan" for this purpose. Check these out for where you live, either by consulting a local financial advisor or researching the matter on the Internet. However, never use these sources of ready cash for *anything other than genuine emergencies*. Taking an overseas vacation is not a "rainy day." If you cannot use any of these methods of saving for the "rainy day," open a savings account into which you pay a fixed amount each month, preferably by standing order. Howard Dayton recommends building this up to three months' income, an excellent amount in my view.

Now try to balance the budget. If you are a high earner, you may find that you are in the happy situation of having a surplus. This is where you need to remember the biblical injunction to "be generous and ready to share" (1 Tim. 6:18). Budget for this sharing activity and then have the sublime pleasure of giving. Remember Jesus's words "It is more blessed to give than to receive"? Try it.

However, I fear that many will experience a shock and discover that they are not living within their means. This is when a family conference is called for and ways and means found to cover the shortfall. First look at every discretionary item and decide which ones can be *eliminated altogether*. This is the most effective way of making large savings. You must be ruthless. Many items which you have regarded as essential may not be that at all. Once you have eliminated some items, you may then look at the size of each item, endeavoring to reduce the amounts budgeted. If all this fails, you must accept that you *simply earn too little* and you must then look for a new job (see Chapter 4). Other members of the family (e.g. wife or teenage children) could also seek employment to boost the family income. I am not advocating that mothers sacrifice their children by working in order to live more affluent lives. In fact, that often does not make economic sense anyway. Howard Dayton cites an example of one wife working hard and the family actually ending up with *less* net income. Some situations will, however, demand that a wife works. If your wife must work to make essential ends meet, try to find an occupation that can be carried out from home or that offers hours which coincide with school hours.

Once you have developed an annual budget, you should break it up into months. Some of the items will occur each month and therefore offer no problem, but others will be "lumpy," such as the annual vacation, annual insurance payments and so on. Also think about the special occasions that occur from time to time, such as a wedding, a special anniversary, a graduation and so on. The best way to show these in your budget is by putting the full amount into the annual column and then dividing it by twelve so that you show a monthly amount. Then transfer the monthly amount to a savings account. You then pay for these items out of the savings account. You must draw up a mini-budget for each of these events as well as including them in the overall family budget.

Finally, you need to control expenditure against the budget. The smart way to do this is by paying for all regular items (including the standing orders into the savings account mentioned above) from a single bank account. Then each month you simply pick up the items from your bank account and transfer them to your spreadsheet as "actuals" which you can compare with your budget. Overspending or negative variances will have to be recovered from the ensuing months, and positive variances can go into savings. Life is generally a bit more complex, as you will probably have credit or debit cards as well; if you do, treat all your means of payment as if they were from a single bank account.

A reminder about credit cards: *never use them for credit*. Pay off your card each month, preferably by direct debit from your bank; in other words, do not build up debt this way. Not only am I opposed to such debt, but also the interest rates are horrific. Nevertheless, credit cards are a useful way of paying (good for Internet purchases) and do offer certain legal protections. On the other hand, debit cards use money directly out of your bank account and avoid the debt trap.

I think that it is important that you go through this exercise at least once to learn how to do it, but after that you may want to rely more heavily on any one of many software packages or online services available to you. In the USA, some of these can be found on the Web sites of Crown Ministries or Dave Ramsey but the best that I found is Mint.[4]

Notes

1 See note 6 in Chapter 1 for details.

2 Dayton, *Your Money Map.*

3 See note 6 in Chapter 1.

4 See note 7 in Chapter 1.

International travel and vacations

M ost people travel abroad on business or vacation. This usually necessitates currency conversions and spending in unfamiliar ways. Once again, you are to act responsibly and as a good steward of your money, and not waste unnecessary funds. Here are a few tips that should help you save money.

All vacations should be included in your annual budget, but before taking an overseas trip (or even a local one), you should make a more detailed budget covering the major items of expenditure on a daily basis. Then, each night of your vacation, compare what you actually spent with your budget. You will either sleep well or know that some belt-tightening is called for. Appendix 3 shows an example of a travel (or vacation) budget. You must decide on the currency that you will use for your budget and against which you will compare actual spending. My advice is to do the daily budget and comparison with the actual expenditure in local currency and then convert to your home currency at the end of each period in a foreign country. Which rate of exchange (ROE) will you use? Clearly the one at which you *bought* your currency. If you have used traveler's checks, use the effective rate after commission; if you have drawn cash at ATMs, try to discover the ROE that you were charged and use the average applying to your various drawings. (Experts can use a money-weighted average.)

Currency

Banks and other money-changers are only too keen to catch unsuspecting travelers by taking a large percentage of their money through the sale of traveler's checks or the conversion of bank notes at airports, railway stations or even in the street. Many businesses will also accept foreign currency. My advice is to beware of all such opportunities to exchange foreign currency. I can understand part of Jesus's anger at seeing the money-changers in the temple; I often feel like that when I see the money-changers' booths. Why my concern?

The rate of exchange such companies offer is invariably very disadvantageous to us. I checked the rates being offered by the British Post Office in mid-2009 and the following is what I found.

If you came into Britain with $1,000 and you called at the Post Office, it would give you £552 based on an exchange rate of $1.8093 = £1. The bank rate (or "spot" rate) at the same time was $1.637 = £1, meaning that on a conversion of $1,000 you lost no less than £59 or $97 (nearly 10 percent)! But that is not all. If you did not need the cash after all and wanted your dollars back, the rate offered was $1.5841 = £1, meaning that your £552 would only give you $875 back; in other words, you would have lost $125 of your $1,000. This is the difference between the "buying" and the "selling" rates. I have used the Post Office as it is probably the most conservative; other booths and banks would probably be worse. So your budget for your foreign trip is probably in error by about 10 percent. How do you avoid being "taken for a ride"?

The best way is to travel with a debit card. Debit cards usually attract a low commission (e.g. 1 percent or less) and can be used to draw money at most ATMs. This is also normally the most convenient way of getting cash. The rate of exchange will normally be the so-called "spot rate" and the transaction will go through your bank in such a way that no advance of cash is involved. You may also pay for goods and services using your credit card, but do not (except in an emergency) use a credit card to draw cash from an ATM. The reason is that there will be a charge for so doing and, in addition, your card-issuing bank will regard the cash as an advance and charge horrific interest from the moment you draw the cash. Be warned that most credit cards also charge anything up to 3 percent commission on foreign *purchases*, thereby inflating the cost of your vacation. But do check these facts with your bank in advance and also inform your card-issuing bank that you will be traveling abroad; otherwise you could find your card being swallowed by the first ATM you use! If in doubt, go into the bank and do a manual withdrawal. In any event, make sure that you carry more than one card in case you have your card swallowed.

Airline tickets

The time has long passed when the price of an airline ticket was firm and all that you needed to do was give your itinerary to your travel agent and he or she would issue you with a correctly priced ticket. Prices can vary enormously from airline to airline and from day to day. While writing this book, I checked the prices on two identical flights separated by a month and found a price difference of over 300 percent (the second flight cost one-third of the price of the first)! I recently needed to get a one-way ticket from London to Knoxville for my granddaughter and found that a one-way ticket cost more than 300 percent the price of a round trip! The moral of the story is simply that you must shop around. The Internet is a perfect marketplace for you to find a good fare. Try the airlines and any of the many consolidators or agents. Many offer a matrix showing the prices over a range of dates that might all suit you. But check the routing. A friend of mine bought the cheapest ticket available only to discover that it took several days zigzagging across North America to reach London. Another tip: when you find the right combination of airline, routing and price, buy the ticket immediately. It will not be available tomorrow. If you cannot get back to what you once saw, you may need to delete cookies from your computer and try again. Finally, buy the ticket at the right time. Any nearer than one week to the flight you will pay a high price. The same is true for a year ahead, when airlines will not be pressed to offer their most competitive prices. Some Internet sites and some airlines offer a "price watch" service and will e-mail you the prices as they fluctuate over your planning period.

Rail or bus passes

Europeans tend to use more public transport than, for example, Americans, South Africans or Australians. Consequently, rail or bus travel is very practical and convenient within Europe, especially when traveling distances less than about 250 miles. Many countries offer rail passes to foreigners which allow flexible travel at very reasonable rates. You can even buy a Eurail Pass, which allows unlimited travel throughout Europe for a fixed period. Do some research on the Internet before you travel, as the savings can be very significant and the convenience of not having to purchase a ticket before each trip is a great time-saver. All these passes have to be bought before you leave your home country.

Expenditure

The old adage "when in Rome do as the Romans do" is still valid when spending money abroad. If you insist on having things the way you had them at home, you will find yourself paying too much. (It also raises the question why you came to a foreign country.) Try to find out what the locals do, where they stay and where they eat. I know of hotels and restaurants in Cape Town that are more or less only frequented by foreigners and they charge London prices. The locals know this and go elsewhere, where prices will be much lower. The same is true throughout the world.

Avoid the souvenir shops, which aim to take as much money as possible off those travelers who consider spending money to be the major joy of a foreign vacation. Do your shopping in the supermarkets and stores where the locals shop. Remember, you are to be a faithful steward and not to waste money.

Insurance

Insurance allows you to pay a relatively small premium to an insurance company so that it takes whatever risk you wish to transfer *away* from yourself *onto* that company. This can apply to your home, your car, your life or your health. In short, it is a "fair exchange," and since there are many insurance companies to choose from, the free market works well.

Insurance is a mystery to many people but should not be so. The basic elements are simple and everyone should understand what they are doing before they buy insurance. Basically, there are two types of insurance: "life," which covers human beings; and what is called "short term," which covers things or situations such as holidays or your health. Let us look at these two classifications in detail.

Short-term insurance

Short-term insurance is very simple and I strongly recommend that you buy it for your car ("comprehensive," which covers everything), your house, your household goods, possibly your health (more of this later) and so on. Shop around; you will be amazed at how low these premiums can be due to the intense competition. Here is a money-saving tip: never attempt to cover what is almost certain to arise, because the insurance company will make sure that you pay for this in full, whatever happens. In short, it will add to your premium the entire amount (plus some profit) of any almost-certain claim. The solution is for you to take a high level of "excess," meaning that you will pay for the first (i.e. the most likely) part of any claim. Insure yourself against the *big risks* that are unlikely and whose premiums are therefore low *but whose consequences could be catastrophic.* In short, insure yourself against that which you cannot afford to lose. A friend of mine once called for quotes for his health insurance. The cost came to the equivalent of $3,000 per year with no excess. He asked for the premium if the excess were $750. The answer was $2,400—$600 less. The insurance company was assuming that there was a 100 percent chance that he would claim $600 every year! He saved $600 immediately, and after about fourteen months of saving on his premium, he could put $750 into a savings account to pay for any excess that might arise in future years. Thereafter, he will be saving $600 per year, every year. This same principle applies to all forms of short-term insurance.

A second money-saving tip: ask a lot of questions beginning, "What if …?" I discovered that if I added my wife's name to my car insurance, the premiums *dropped*! A friend recently told me that when he increased the miles that he drove every year, his premiums *dropped*! I am sure an actuary could explain this, but frankly you and I do not need to know the reason why. Keep asking for all the combinations until you find the lowest premium from a respectable company.

The UK has the National Health Service, so for British residents it is not strictly necessary to take out private health insurance. But you may prefer the benefits of private health care, in which case you should take out private health insurance. There are two types. With the first, you pay a flat rate related to your age regardless of whether or not you make any claims. The other type offers an increasing "no-claims bonus" for each year in which you make no claim (rather like car insurance); should you make a claim, your premiums will rise, often becoming higher than the first type. If you perceive that your health risks are such that you will make no claims until near your death, then clearly the "no-claims bonus" type will be preferable. Otherwise, take the former type.

In countries with no government health service, it is very important that you take health insurance for yourself and your family. It may even be offered as a benefit by your employer. In some cases, you may be able to join without restrictions on prior conditions and may be permitted to change your insurer without new conditions. When determining the benefits of these schemes, do not imagine that money grows on trees and that your insurer will pay for everything you are likely to encounter. Some sensible exclusions are advisable. It is virtually certain that you will visit a doctor at least once a year, so if you try to insure yourself against this risk, you will discover that the insurance company will simply add the full cost of visiting the doctor (plus a profit) to your annual premium. You had best cover these routine visits from your own pocket. Some health insurance policies establish a savings scheme within the policy and you can then use these savings to pay for routine expenses. Insure yourself *against the big risks*: an operation, a heart attack, cancer and so on.

Life insurance

Life insurance is aimed at having a company take over the risk of you dying sooner than the average life expectancy or becoming disabled and so on. It is a good idea, and I think a biblical case can be made for it from 1 Timothy 5:8: "But if anyone does not provide for his relatives, and especially for members of his household, he has denied the faith and is worse than an unbeliever." Surely the provision should outlive the breadwinner?

Certain types of insurance—endowment policies—are often sold as a combination of insurance and investment. The sales pitch is that you should get something back for all the money that you pay out in insurance. This is complete nonsense because all that an endowment policy comprises is a term life policy (hopefully at the usual premium) and a mutual fund investment, both of which you can buy separately (more about this below). The real reason for the salesperson's enthusiasm for endowment-type policies (whatever they may be called) is the enormous commission paid—often to the value of one or more years of your premiums. So *keep insurance and savings separate*, as I illustrate in the next chapter. "Term life insurance" (insurance for a fixed period) and "whole life insurance" (paid out when you die) are simple and subject to considerable competition. The commissions are low, so most of the premium goes into providing you with insurance.

My counsel is that the breadwinner in every family must take sufficient "term insurance" to cover the vulnerable period of his or her life, and perhaps some whole life insurance. The amount of term insurance must be sufficient to produce an income that replaces the breadwinner's earnings for the critical periods of his or her life—for example, when children are still at school or college. We will consider values in the case study below. If you cannot afford the premiums on this policy, "insure your insurability": take "health protection insurance" that will allow you to purchase the insurance at a later date without any further medical examinations. However, note that you will be putting your family at risk in the meantime.

Permanent or partial disability

Some employers will insure their employees under a low-cost group scheme, covering them in the event of an accident or illness that makes them unfit for work for a period or permanently. Check this with your employer. If you do not enjoy such insurance, I strongly recommend that you buy at least the same amount as you need to cover an untimely death (see case study below). The problem caused by your inability to work would be the same or even worse than that caused by your death, as you would still be living and might incur additional expenses due to your disability. These policies are sometimes linked to a life policy and should also cover you for a long period of unemployment due to accident or illness.

Funeral insurance

Policies to pay for funeral expenses are simply a form of "whole life" insurance policies—ones which pay out a fixed sum (or an escalating sum) on your death. The advantage of these schemes is that the payout goes directly to the funeral home and, in some jurisdictions, may not even form part of your estate. However, they are no different from any other whole life policies and may well cost a lot more. The main advantage accrues to the funeral home, which gets paid promptly!

Some pensioners are attracted to these policies even though their monthly incomes are modest. I can see little point as your funeral can be paid from your estate; there is no need to make life more difficult while you are still alive.

Example: How much insurance?

Suppose you are a father, thirty years old, earn $2,500 per month after tax and have bought your own home worth $250,000. You borrowed $50,000 from your parents (which they probably do not want repaid) and have taken a mortgage of $200,000 for the balance of the purchase of the house. You have no other debt. Your wife stays at home to care for your children aged six and four. What insurance do you need?

We can assume that your children will need support for a maximum of twenty years, so you should buy sufficient level term insurance to generate an income that will replace your salary for that period. Should you die at any time during those twenty years, the only costs that will fall away are those associated with you (your food, transport, clothes, etc.). Assume that your expenses are $500 per month and that this will fall away when you die. Your wife will therefore need an income of about $2,000 (after tax) per month but rising over the years to compensate for inflation. To generate this sort of income and completely use up the capital over the twenty years, she would need to invest about $400,000 if you died tomorrow. The worst case must cover your family from the first day, but as the years roll on, so the figure decreases. For example, after ten years, you will only need about $250,000 of cover. Consequently, you could take $250,000 for the full twenty years (more of this later) and an extra $150,000 for the first ten years. Clearly, you can calculate more finely than this and cover your life in five-year intervals, starting at $400,000 for the first five years and decreasing by $50,000 every five years. But you need to increase all of these amounts to compensate for inflation, so it may well revert to the $400,000. In addition, after the twenty years your wife will have *nothing*, so you need to increase the amount of insurance to cover an income of, say, $1,000 per month for the rest of her life. As you may die after twenty years have passed, you need to make some insurance "whole life," meaning that it continues until the day you die. How much should that be? Once the children are off your wife's hands and the house is paid off, she may only need about $250,000 to generate the $1,000 per month. This will depend on her age. The outcome of all this is to suggest that the $400,000 term cover (maybe reducing in steps) needs to be supplemented by something like $250,000 whole life cover. All of this can be reduced if your wife can continue to earn an income, will receive a widow's pension or enjoy some state welfare support.

A word of caution. Your mortgage provider will no doubt want you to hold insurance for the value of the mortgage which will pay off the mortgage: in other words, they will want you to take out insurance for an initial value of $200,000. Superficially, it would seem that this could be covered by the $250,000 whole life insurance proposed above. But the mortgage provider will think differently and will want the mortgage paid off on your death, leaving your wife with too little to generate an income on which to live. As she will enjoy a fully paid-for house, she may cope, but more likely she will need the life cover of $250,000 as well.

You may have established a lifestyle which needs more than the $2,500 per month base that I worked on, in which case you should increase all the figures accordingly. Figures for the UK and other countries will need to be calculated along the same lines. The above is meant as an example only, but as income, costs of living, tax rates and level of welfare support differ materially for each family and from country to country, you need to do a careful analysis for your own case. You may need a financial advisor to give you a hand, but remember, pay for his or her advice, and do not accept final advice from anyone who stands to gain from that advice.

Saving and providing for a pension

A ll of us must be responsible about providing for our old age. This will entail saving, which is commended in Proverbs 13:11: "Wealth gained hastily will dwindle, but whoever gathers little by little will increase it." (This is not to say that we are to look forward to a life of luxury and ease in which we do not work—that, in my view, is unbiblical.) The task is not straightforward and there are no guarantees. This is one of the lessons from Chapter 3. We are grateful to God for his grace in providing the world with well-developed financial systems, but, as we have seen in the financial crisis since 2007, human depravity damages the best of institutions. Our task as faithful stewards is not necessarily to become financial experts, but we should at least understand what we are doing and, when we call in the experts, ask the correct questions. Detailed knowledge in any profession is always valuable, but there is nothing in family finances which cannot be understood by anyone who can count. Do not let the mystique which surrounds this subject mislead you, and do not let anyone bamboozle you with fancy terminology. There is an old saying that "where there is mystery, there is money." The financial industry thrives on mystery in order to make unjustified profits. Beware!

The first principle to grasp about the provision of a pension is that *money does not grow on trees*! All that you will get back as a pension is what you have put into the scheme in the first place, plus some growth. There is nothing "magical" about any pension scheme, with one exception. Government schemes are generally "pay as you go," in which the current contributors pay for the pensioners. Governments believe that they can work this way because they will never get to the end of employing current contributors (usually in growing numbers as well!). Companies are forced to think differently because some pensioners may (and sometimes do) outlast the company. Even though your employer may also contribute to your pension, this is just an efficient tax method of paying you. It is always *your* savings plus returns which are "rolled up," so that when you do finally go on pension, there is a substantial amount available for you to unwind during your pension years. As you will see, there are some wrinkles to this, but the principle remains: you will *only get back what you have put in.*

Here I must repeat some very important advice. If you do not feel able to handle the details of any investment, consult a professional. But *never take any final advice from someone who stands to gain from that advice.* Such a person will lure you by pointing out that his or her advice is "free." Nothing is ever "free"; someone always pays and, in the case of salespeople (whatever their title), the financial institution will pay them a commission. Where do you think the financial institution gets the money to pay the commission? From you! So, if you plan to allow someone to sell financial products to you, by all means listen to that person's ideas, but hire an *independent advisor* to guide you in your *final decisions.* Make sure that these two people act independently of each other.

It may be that if you work for a stable government or some large and well-managed company, you will have a final salary pension which will be adequate to support you and your spouse to the end of your lives. To test whether or not any scheme is adequate, look at the total amount invested each year. If the scheme invests some 15–20 percent of your income over a very long period and in a well-managed way, you may be provided for. Just one word of caution. If your pension will come from a company-run final-salary scheme, check the stability of the scheme and of the company. Size is not the key issue. Some of the largest companies in the world have underfunded pension schemes (e.g. General Motors in the USA and Royal Mail in the UK), and sometimes the company itself will not be able to warrant the pension (e.g. General Motors). You need only read on if you wish to supplement your scheme or if you need to create a pension for yourself.

A reminder before you start to save. I have already shown that you should not borrow and save at the same time. *You are not actually saving until you have paid off all loans,* so pay off your debts as a matter of urgency. Perhaps this is the time to return to Chapter 5 and read about debt. The number one tip for starting saving is therefore to *clear all your short-term debts*. Then concentrate on paying off your mortgage as fast as you can. From a purely economic perspective, a case can be made for paying off your mortgage *entirely* before you commence saving for a pension at all; however, I do not advise this because it puts too much of your savings into one asset.

Investments

When looking for a "safe" investment, the golden rule is to spread your risks because *nothing is safe*.

You must diversify by putting some money into equities (shares), some into property and some into cash or cash equivalents, such as bonds. This may be too much effort for you; in that case, find an investment portfolio that spreads your savings over these three areas. Or, more prudently, find *several* portfolios with different institutions. Recent collapses of the largest banks (e.g. Lehman Brothers) and the largest investment houses demonstrate the insecurity of *all* institutions. Moreover, you must consider inflation. In the Western world we have been lulled into a false sense of security about inflation because we have known a long period of low inflation. However, the policy of governments to print money must lead to higher inflation unless huge productivity gains can be made, and that is unlikely, given that most countries will simultaneously follow expensive energy policies in an attempt to limit carbon emissions. It is good stewardship to do the best you can, but remember: in the final analysis we are not to trust in our riches, but in God. He never fails. We must be good and faithful stewards but must not *worry* about our investments (Matt. 6:34).

You may be overwhelmed by the terminology and the concepts, so let me try to boil all investments down to their simplest forms (with apologies to professionals in the industry). Basically, you can invest in one of two ways. Firstly, you can invest at a fixed or semi-fixed return which is guaranteed and is usually in the form of interest or a dividend (which may have different tax treatments). Generally, this is in a bank, "thrift" or building society, government bonds and so on. Secondly, you can invest in something that does not produce a guaranteed income and, even worse, may cause you to lose your original capital as well. This investment could be in property, shares, commodities, derivatives, futures and the like. While these are more risky, they offer potentially higher returns and also tend to track inflation. We will look at each of these components separately.

PROPERTY

One of the advantages of property is that it tends to follow inflation, achieving one of your goals. But a disadvantage is that its value may rise and fall in short-term cycles and it may be difficult to sell during some periods. It is therefore said to be "illiquid."

The most obvious investment in property is your family home. This is one of the reasons why I recommend that you own a house and pay off the mortgage as soon as you can. Further investments in property can either be "direct," in that you could purchase another property, or "indirect," if you invest in a property trust, known as known as a Real Estate Investment Trust (REIT) in the USA. REITs offer reasonable returns as they are required by law to pay out 90 percent of their profits in dividends. A direct investment could be a house, an apartment, or a commercial building. You rent it out and pay off any mortgage from the rent received, supplemented, perhaps, from your own income. This can be rewarding but it is hard work and is not for everyone. Alternatively, you can join forces with others in what is known as a property syndicate and own a portion of whatever portfolio the syndicate invests in. The key issue in all direct property investments is to buy the right properties at the right prices and in the right areas, which calls for knowledge which you may or may not have. Do not attempt it without knowledge or very sound advice. Also, make sure that there is a way out (the "exit") when you want your cash. Another form of property investment that may suit your needs is a holiday home; you and your family can then derive benefit from its use as well. But be careful; appreciation on these "luxuries" is often not as good as with normal residential homes or commercial property. My advice is that if you do wish to do this, buy a property which is not strictly a holiday house but can be used as normal accommodation as well. It will then produce "normal" appreciation.

What about timeshare? Timeshare is never an investment and should not be seen as part of your investment portfolio. If you do buy timeshare as part of your *vacation planning*, make sure that it does not lock you and your estate into perpetual levies. Some schemes do, so beware. You cannot *give* them away. Also, be aware that a huge amount of your payment is absorbed into very lavish upfront marketing and high-pressure selling costs. This all goes down the drain as soon as you buy! Timeshare is consumption spending.

An "indirect" method of linking some of your investment to property is through shares in a property trust. These are investment companies that specialize in property and have the knowledge referred to above. Growth tends to be stable and returns are mid-range. If you choose a mutual fund as set out under "Stock exchanges" below, make sure you select one that includes property in the portfolio.

BANKS

The safest investment, but most volatile in terms of returns, is in a bank or thrift (building society), or credit union. Interest rates can, and will, vary substantially so that your income will move up and down, often by large amounts. My wife earns interest on her bank investments and over the 2008/09 recession her income *more than halved* as interest rates tumbled. She still has her capital, and no doubt rates will improve again, but had she relied on this source alone for her income, she would have been using up capital. Make sure your investment in any one bank never exceeds the value of the government-guaranteed amount (in 2010 this was $250,000 in the USA and £50,000 in the UK). Also, avoid banks from smaller countries (e.g. Iceland and Ireland), where the government guarantee is worthless because the government does not have the credit rating to cover its obligations.

Remember that for any investment, the higher the return, the higher the risk. Do not be tempted by any high-return investments. What do I mean by "high return"? A good benchmark for a fair return is the basic rate set by the central bank (Federal Reserve, Bank of England, etc.). A poor rate will be lower than the central bank rate and a good rate will be slightly above it. But beware of anything which is more than a few percentage points above these rates.

BONDS

Bonds are useful, secure, long-term investment vehicles that give a modest return and will sometimes be tax-free (as municipal bonds are in the USA) and are therefore of value to those with high incomes. There are many different types of bonds, such as variable interest rate bonds, partial redemption bonds and so on. For simplicity I will describe bonds in general; if you want more detail, information can be found on the Internet.

Government bonds are issued by various levels of government as a means of obtaining finance for long-term projects or even for consumption expenditure. They are the means whereby governments balance their books when they overspend against their revenues (regrettably a common phenomenon, as described in Chapter 2). While bonds are also issued by companies, I am not recommending that you invest in bonds other than those issued by stable governments, councils or municipalities and which are also highly rated. Various agencies (e.g. Standard & Poor's, Moody's, etc.) award "A," "AA" or "AAA" ratings, with "AAA" being the highest. Bonds are sometimes also insured, thereby increasing their security even further. They are issued at a face value and usually a fixed interest rate over the term. These values (also known as "coupon values") usually result in terms of twenty, thirty or even fifty years, with interest rates typically in the 4–5 percent p.a. range. Interest will be paid at regular intervals (quarterly or half-yearly), but the bond cannot normally be cashed before its maturity date. However, it can be sold. So, if you invest in a bond for thirty years and want your money back sooner, you can sell it on one of the bond markets attached to stock markets around the world. The question is, what will you get for a bond which is somewhere along its life? That is entirely market related. During times of high interest rates, the bond will be unattractive because the interest rates are relatively modest, so if you sell the bond you will receive less than the face value (lose capital value). However, if interest rates have dropped, as they did in 2009, then even the modest interest rate may be attractive so the bond may sell *above* its face value. Indeed, you may have bought it at a discounted price and then discover that its resale value has appreciated. Most investment portfolios will contain some bonds, but you can also purchase them privately. Bonds are more secure than shares but are less easy to trade.

STOCK EXCHANGES

The stock exchange is a market where capital can be raised by companies and the public can invest money. There is nothing wrong with that in theory. A problem, however, arises from the nature of how the whole system *actually* operates, which is nearer to a gamble than a careful assessment of the investment opportunities. Gambling is not work and therefore not appropriate for a Christian.

Most of the movement of cash in any stock exchange is done by large investors—usually the mutual funds, insurance companies or pension funds, known as "institutional investors"—using the funds that we contribute every month (e.g. for our pensions). A large number of small transactions are also carried out by the public, often on a "day trade" basis, buying and selling as soon as a gain is made and often quite regardless of the underlying value of the share. On the one hand, these traders are beneficial, as they tend to make the exchange more of a genuine market, driven by the public. On the other hand, their trading habits are seldom driven by knowledge. They merely follow the prevailing market, which, as we shall see, is driven by itself and not necessarily by facts or predictions. Consequently, when a share is rising, everyone buys it, thereby chasing its price ever higher without regard to any logic which may indicate that it is overpriced. Then something triggers a reduction in the share price and a suicidal "lemmings rush" commences, with everyone dumping the shares as the price tumbles, causing it to drop even faster. The entire market becomes a gamble, with "investors" playing the familiar game of "chicken" (perhaps "Russian roulette" would be more appropriate) on the rising market.

To return to the institutional investors: the institutions employ "investment advisors," "share pickers" and "asset managers." These people invest that portion of your chosen fund in listed shares. They are trained to do financial analysis and endeavor to determine the value of any share. Many do a good job, and, in addition to looking at balance sheets, cash flow and other historic financial data, will sometimes investigate the market, the company's position in this market, the quality of management, technology, marketing expertise and so on. But all too often, all "investment science" is ignored and they merely follow the market up and down, much like the day traders, contributing to the unstable situation described above. Their behavior is driven by the knowledge that investors do not admire asset managers who do a thorough analysis but produce short-term results that are less than those of other asset managers who simply buy in a rising market and sell in a falling market, showing wonderful "paper" returns. Really astute investors will withdraw before the share (or the entire market) collapses and will then hold cash until the next upswing. But very few ever achieve this because they are loath to miss any growth, and greed for their bonuses drives them on. Asset managers receive massive bonuses (often seven figures or more) for beating a benchmark return (usually the average of all funds), *even when the shares go down.* When the market goes up, they take the credit (and get a massive bonus) for making profit for their fund, but when it goes down, they simply blame the market for collapsing; provided that they lose less than others, they will still get a bonus. We saw this happening between 2007 and 2009.

What suddenly causes a share price to escalate or drop and trigger this whole unstable situation? Sometimes real valid news, such as that of a new chief executive or a technological breakthrough, or some external news such as war, a hurricane or a change in national politics. Often, however, it is a rumor which rightly or wrongly sparks a rising price or a drop. All of this gives rise to huge pressure for a company to continually produce good news (or good rumors), which is usually code for rising profits, sales or number of customers, regardless of whether this is true or not. Hence the propensity to overstate balance-sheet values, as happened in the banking crisis of 2007/08. Accounting standards may be bent or reports falsified. Recent examples that received a great deal of coverage in the media were Enron and their now defunct auditors Arthur Andersen, WorldCom and Tyco. All three had found ways of presenting financial data which misled the investing public and the banks to such an extent that, when the collapses came, the companies broke records for bankruptcies! It is worth noting that nine out of ten investment advisors were still advising investors to buy Enron shares a week before the collapse! More recently, we have seen the large US and UK banks floundering because debt which they had created (see Chapter 2) turned out to be worthless. In all these situations, the accountants and auditors were signing off profits and balance sheets which did not reflect the true situation. As just one example, the Royal Bank of Scotland (RBS) was forced to write off £28 billion because its balance sheet contained huge but worthless debts (the largest write-down in British banking history). The building up of these debts had earned the bank's executives massive bonuses and inflated the share price! The same story emerged for US banks such as Lehman Brothers. When the UK government nationalized Northern Rock, shareholders expected compensation. They will get none because they had invested in a worthless company that had been led by management that placed greed above caution. Investing in public-listed shares is never secure. Few of the highly paid asset managers spotted that the shares of RBS and Northern Rock were in fact worthless. The shares of RBS actually fell by 97 percent over the crisis between 2007 and 2009. Who lost in all these failures? The investing public and pensioners. People like you and me. Who gained? The overpaid executives who still collected their huge bonuses and pensions.

Why have I set all this out? In part, to emphasize that, while the stock market is a legitimate place for companies to raise funds and the public to invest funds, it must be well understood by anyone who uses it directly or indirectly. Do not gamble on the stock exchange. I also want to illustrate the dangers of placing too much trust in stock markets. Salespeople will try to convince you to invest through their organizations by producing graphs and tables showing the year-on-year growth of their stock-market-linked products. They will emphasize that, in the long term, stock markets do perform well; in fact, on average, they outperform most other investments. But what they do not show you are the fluctuations from day to day. They will dismiss these on the basis that you are making a long-term investment. That is true, but what if you happen to invest all your money on a *day* when the market is very high and it then collapses immediately thereafter? You would simply lose, and it could take decades for you to catch up with a simple savings account. This happens on a regular basis. I have seen it happen at least five times during the period that I have been interested in financial matters. One way around this problem is to spread your entry into the market over a period, say the entire year. That way you effectively buy in at the *average annual* price. But there are even better ways, which I set out below. (In fairness, it is also true that you could also make a windfall profit if you bought on a low and sold on a high, but that is gambling.)

The way I advise people to invest in the stock market is over a very long time with a *more-or-less-fixed amount* being invested every month—or one which only changes slowly. Your pension (in whatever form it may be) and any investment component of an insurance policy effectively do just that. The reason why this is good is because you get the benefits of what is called "dollar cost averaging," "pound cost averaging," "Euro cost averaging" and so on. Investing the *same amount of money* each month ensures that, when the market is low, you buy more shares (or units, if your investment is in a mutual fund) so that, when the market swings up again, you have more shares to gain value. The converse is also true; when the market is high, you buy fewer shares so that, when the market falls, you lose less. Even if the market swings up and down and ends up where it started, you will own more low-cost shares to grow in value on every upswing than you own to lose on the downswings. Amazing but true. So a stable monetary value invested over a very long time (decades) is a good idea. It is worth mentioning that, when you get near to the time when you intend withdrawing from the market, you must do the same thing in reverse or else you may find that you withdraw on a "low" day (more of this below).

Perhaps you have a lump sum which has come from an inheritance or sale of a property, for example. How do you invest it and be a good steward, even if losing it will not be a disaster? The golden rule is *never to invest a lump sum in anything linked to the stock market.* As an illustration, if you had invested your lump sum early in 2001, you would have lost 30–40 percent of it within the first two years (maybe more if you had hit a bad day). It would only have regained its value by early 2007 (just in time to collapse by 40 percent again). It will take very good performance to recover the loss and then still give you a positive return within, say, ten years. So what do you do? You will see various schemes advertised called by exotic names or even "bonds." They will guarantee your capital and then give you something like 50 percent of the growth of a stock market index. Sounds good, but you can do this yourself and get *100 percent of the growth*! Here is how. Take the lump sum and place it in the best long-term interest (or dividend) earning investment you can find which will pay interest regularly (say monthly or quarterly). This will usually be in a bank or even a bond (see above). Then use *that* monthly income to buy units in the mutual fund of your choice on a "dollar (or pound etc.) cost averaging" basis. If possible, do this on an automatic payment order. These monthly investments will produce a good return even if the stock exchange bounces around. Only if the stock exchange goes into a protracted slide, and does not recover before you want the cash, will the results be poor—but they will never be nothing. In reality, the long-term slide has never happened. The declines are always fairly sharp and then produce substantial returns when the market recovers. The 2001 slide did continue until 2003, but even this is "short" if we are looking at an investment lasting decades. Your capital is also protected as it is in a safe savings account.

We can now move on to see how to use these various options to create a long-term savings plan which could be the basis of your pension or an addition to it.

Pensions

I found this very clear definition of a "pension" on the Prudential Web site:

A pension is simply a form of saving for retirement that has generous tax benefits. The money you save in a pension builds up into a pot which is invested and when you elect to take your benefits the pot is used to pay a regular taxable income for life. You can also choose a lump sum payment and a reduced pension if you wish.[1]

There are basically two types of pension. One is a genuine pension provided by an employer. It will probably be referred to as a "defined benefit plan" or "final salary plan." The pension is based on final income and years of service with the company, regardless of what has actually been paid in or how well the fund has performed. If the fund has been well invested and the amount in the fund exceeds what is needed to pay all pensions, we say the fund is "in surplus," but this may not translate into a higher pension; the pension is simply safer. However, in recent years, due to stock-market collapses and poor investments on the part of the asset managers, many company pension funds are "underfunded," that is, they do not have enough cash to pay their pension obligations. According to a report by the BBC on August 5, 2009, the pension funds of the top 100 companies in the UK had a combined "underfunding" of £96 billion. A similar situation has occurred in the USA (General Motors, now in bankruptcy, has a severely underfunded pension fund. IBM [UK] have announced plans to terminate their pension scheme). It is therefore a major problem and is likely to affect many people. Pensioners and even employees who are still to go on pension are therefore at risk and may not be paid the pension they expect. In many cases, all is not lost because these funds are underwritten by the company itself; in other words, the employer will pay in if necessary because the pension is at the *employer's risk*. But what if the employer cannot pay or has already gone bankrupt (as nearly happened with GM in the USA)? This has happened in many cases, leaving pensioners with the risk of a reduced or even a lost pension. The employees are therefore ultimately at risk after all, which brings us to the second type of pension.

This second scheme is known as a "defined contribution scheme." In the USA, it is called a "401(k)," and elsewhere a "provident fund," an "annuity" or "superannuation." This is really a savings scheme with some tax incentives. Whether or not your employer contributes or simply pays you a higher salary and you pay the scheme is determined by tax considerations. The upside of this method is that you get the full value of the fund, and, if your fund performs well, you may end up with a better-than-expected pension. The downside, however, is that *you are taking the risk*, and if the fund performs badly, you will get a lower-than-expected pension. In recent years, both employers and employees have chosen to move to these defined contribution schemes because they have come to realize that the employer may not be able to guarantee the pension when the time comes. In these cases, the employee still ends up being at risk so he or she may as well also enjoy any "upside." I suspect that, apart from those run by governments, true pension schemes are dead.

If you think that your employer's scheme will give you sufficient income when you become a pensioner, you need do nothing further. However, I recommend that you do some calculations because in most cases it will not. How much should you be putting away? We can work this out now.

Suppose you work for thirty years and think that you will live for thirty years after you go on pension. Ignoring any growth in your savings, and assuming that you want the same income throughout your life, it is very simple to see that you will need to save half your income when you are working. You live on half now and then the other half during the second half of your life. But this is a ridiculous case, serving only to give us the upper limit of saving 50 percent of your income.

Instead, suppose that you think you will live only for twenty-five years after pension; then you need only save twenty-five divided by thirty (equal to five-sixths) of half your income, or about 40 percent. But suppose you also think that, at that time, you will have paid off your house, will have no children dependent on you and will possibly live a quieter life; you may then only want an income of about half the average of your salary. You then only need to save about 20 percent of your salary. Inflation will require you to save slightly more but this should be more than offset by growth in your fund so that you need save only about 15–18 percent, provided that you do so all your working life. If you start later, you will need to move to a higher figure, and vice versa. (Senior executives who join a company in later life need to contribute about 70 percent of their income to provide a good pension.) Check what you are doing and, if necessary, top up. Naturally, this is a very rough guide but it is the figure most advisors will come up with and you can see why. Clearly, you may need less if you already have a large amount already saved or are expecting an inheritance or other lump sum. Maybe you own a lot of equity in your home; it is very much part of your retirement planning. When you need to, you can sell your family home and buy something smaller, putting the surplus into your pension fund. Regrettably in the UK, paying off your mortgage has negative results, such as disqualifying you from certain benefits and raising your net assets at death, thereby possibly attracting inheritance tax. But these are other considerations and can be dealt with in various ways beyond the scope of this book. Finally, you may be able to claim a state pension which will reduce the amount that you need to save for a pension.

Another matter to remember is that some pension schemes come by other names. Do you have any endowment insurance? This is essentially a pension plan that will produce a lump-sum benefit at some time of your choosing, usually around when you plan to go on pension. In general, I do not advise endowment insurance for this purpose because a very large part (one to two years of your premiums) is paid in commission to the agent. However, there may be tax advantages, so this needs to be checked with an independent advisor (not the salesperson!).

Suppose you decide to top up your pension plan, or maybe you have no scheme and need to do it all yourself. How best can you do it?

You will easily find a host of "financial advisors" who will give you free advice and want to sell you amazing products that will make you rich some day. Beware of greed (yours and theirs)! You will be shown graphs of amazing performances and all you have to do is sign and start paying. I did that some forty years ago, and guess what? I was the advisor and I believed all my own sales talk. During the last few years I have been paid out from all these policies and none of them produced results that even beat a Post Office savings account! Remember what I said earlier: *never take final advice from anyone who stands to gain from his or her advice*. If he or she is a salesperson by some other name, use that person as such, but seek independent advice and pay for it.

At this point I recommend that you re-read the section on "dollar (or pound etc.) cost averaging" set out above. The point of this is that you must never put any lump sum into the stock exchange but only use the stock exchange for very long-term investments, with a more-or-less constant amount invested each month. Putting a percentage of your income into a stock-market-linked fund every month is ideal for this purpose. A stock market fund which spreads risk over a number of shares and other assets such as property and bonds is variously called a "managed fund," a "mutual fund," a "unit trust" or, in Australia, a "superannuation fund." "Index funds" or "tracker funds" are funds which purchase shares in the same ratio as the particular stock exchange index that you are buying, for example, the Dow Jones index in the USA or the FTSE 100 index in England. They have generally outperformed the managed funds (apologies to fund managers for whom this is not true). A further problem with managed funds is the difficulty in choosing one, as you have no way of determining what they are likely to do *in the future* whatever they may have achieved in the past. Buying an index-linked fund means that you will get a return which is the same as the growth in the *whole* market, thus eliminating the judgment of the asset managers. However, your investment is not guaranteed and you will find such a disclaimer on many of the Web sites of the funds themselves. Your units will decrease in value if the whole market collapses (as it did as recently as 1987, 2001 and 2007).

How do you know which fund to invest in? You can get some idea about reputation and performance by reading the financial press and asking someone who *will not get a commission* from advising you. If you choose an index-linked fund, you should look at the costs associated with the fund (known as the "loading"). Clearly, lowering the costs (or loading) will leave more of your money to invest. The next problem is to find a low-cost way of buying units in these funds. Try your bank. Alternatively, do some research on the Internet. You want to avoid a broker who creams off a substantial percentage before your money ever gets to the fund. A 5 percent upfront commission or a 0.25 percent ongoing commission may not sound a lot but if your fund only produces a 7 percent gain p.a. (which is good long term), then you are giving most of the first year's income away. Key things to look for are commission costs, expense costs and reputation in the market.

When you go on pension

A day will arrive when you will no longer enjoy any earned income (although I trust that you do not stop "working") and will live off your pension. You may well have an adequate pension and need do nothing further. If this is true for you, good, but you are in the minority, as most people are in for a nasty surprise. This calls for action now by those who have not yet reached pension age (see above), but for those who have reached pension age, it calls for special care. The first action must start *about five years before you plan to go on pension*. If you have been "dollar cost averaging," you will understand the importance of investing over a long period. The reverse is now true; you must *unwind your investment over a long period of time* as well. If you wait to *withdraw* all your savings on a single day, you may select a poor day and lose a substantial amount. Consider the falls of 2001 and 2008. In both cases, worldwide markets suddenly fell by about 40 percent and your pension would have gone down the same amount. Even the smartest fund managers suffered losses despite seeing trouble coming, and they failed to convert most of their holdings into cash. The index funds simply crash with the market. The best fund I know about managed to hold its losses to 8 percent over this period, *but it was still a loss.*

You must change the "risk profile" of your investments during the five years before you go on pension, converting your accumulated assets into cash or other protected assets over the final five years, ready for you to consider what to do next. Ironically, many people take this sum and put it back precisely where it has just come from and, in the process, give the agents a second set of commissions! Please do not do that; read on for advice.

You must invest your savings in a way that will create a safe and steady income, with or without inflation adjustments. Once again, beware the eager salespeople who will offer to help. Many will have good ideas and will be good, sincere and knowledgeable people—but who drive fancy cars. They make large commissions, so *pay for advice from someone who does not stand to gain from it.* In most tax jurisdictions, you can take a portion (typically 25–33 percent) of your accumulated pension out in cash. Full details of your choices are given by most insurance or investment companies (e.g. on the Prudential Web site: pru.co.uk; note that I have no personal connection with Prudential!). Here are some of the broad-brush ways you should consider.

- One way is for you to take all or part of the capital and invest in several places in very secure income-earning assets, such as savings accounts in several major banks. The problem with this solution is that it will result in a variable income as interest rates move up and down, and it will not compensate for inflation.
- Another way is to invest in a property which produces income, or in a property trust which produces a steady dividend stream.
- The stock market will also offer shares which generate high-dividend streams, and your advisor will be able to help you find these. You can also leave some money in a mutual fund and then sell some of the fund every month regardless of what underlying growth takes place.

- Another possibility is to place the money with an insurance fund that will do all the likely analysis of how long you may live, what income it can expect on your money and so. The company will then offer you a guaranteed income for life, with or without inflation adjustments. This is the best option for those who want to pass all the risks onto an insurance company (which is what insurance companies are there for), but it is possible to do the same calculation yourself, and perhaps you are happy to take both the risk and the profit. The necessary formulas are available on MS Excel. If you use an insurance company, be sure to get competitive quotes, as they will vary considerably.
- Please do what I call a "lunacy test." Assume that on the day you wish to go on pension you will have a lump sum of, say, $500,000. Assume that you are sixty-five and therefore are likely to live another seventeen years or 204 months. If you put this money under your bed and brought out an equal amount every month, you would have a "pension" of about $2,500 per month. This is the minimum that any insurance company should offer you, but it suffers from three problems: 1. it assumes that no interest is earned on the outstanding amount while the capital lies under your bed (a bad place for it to be; what would Jesus say about that?); 2. the income remains constant in the face of inflation; and 3. when you reach eighty-two you will run out of income. What if you live to 102? In reality, you will invest the lump sum wisely and it will produce income and growth. Provided that this is above inflation (which it should be), you can enjoy a larger income *and* one which can even grow at the inflation rate. However, you have to deal with the possibility of living beyond eighty-two. This is where the insurance company comes in. It knows the probability of you living less than eight-two years and of you living beyond that. It calculates these risks and deducts some of the income to pay for the risk. You should still get more than $2,500 per month with increases to offset inflation.
- Invest in your family. This is a method often overlooked by parents. Generally, elderly people have capital, no debt and no income, whereas their adult children usually have steady incomes but no capital and probably mortgages on their homes. The parents will be

struggling to get a *high* interest rate whereas the children will be struggling to find a *low* interest rate. The difference between the two is the profit made by the bank. So why not lend your children the capital to finance their homes and share the interest saved and won? You can even donate to your children and then have them donate a monthly amount back to you. This will avoid income tax on your interest earnings; however, the donation may give rise to gift (or donations) tax, and in the UK will give rise to inheritance tax if you die within seven years of making the donation. On the other hand, in some tax jurisdictions you may discover that a portion of a donation to an elderly parent is *deductible from taxable income*! So, in addition to gaining at the expense of the bank, you may even gain in tax. If you lend the money to your children, it will not give rise to any gift tax, and on your death they will inherit the loan (the loan will be wiped out). The optimum may be a combination of donations and loans. (I recommend that you go back and re-read the paragraphs on tax.)

Inheritance

Do not forget to make a will. In some countries, without a will you may find that your estate will be placed in a trust and not be available to your dependants for a long time, bringing them real hardship. Drawing up a will is an easy exercise and can be done with the help of many agencies or legal experts at modest cost.

One of the four legitimate ways of gaining wealth is through inheritance. This is entirely biblical, and inheritance rules are set out several times in the Old Testament. Here is one word of wisdom from Proverbs: "A good man leaves an inheritance to his children's children ..." (13:22). Your responsibility to be a good steward does not end when you die. You should plan your affairs so that you minimize all costs and taxes on your death. I find death taxes (inheritance tax) particularly lacking in morality because much of what you have accumulated will be from money that has already been taxed. It also destroys wealth. The Swiss have a good solution: provided you leave your assets to your family, they are free from death taxes. In this way, wealth is preserved in families, thereby reducing the burden on the state to look after you and your descendants. However, in most countries, your estate could end up paying a very large percentage of your assets in taxes. Once again, I advise you to consult a professional in this field and pay for his or her services; do not accept final advice from anyone who stands to gain from that advice.

Note

1 From "What is a Pension?" within the "Pensions Guide" at: pru.co.uk. This entire site is very useful for UK readers. US readers should refer to Crown Financial Ministries at: crown.org.

Training your children: pocket money and allowances

The Bible teaches, "Fathers ... bring them [children] up in the discipline and instruction of the Lord" (Eph. 6:4). Part of this training is in the use and handling of money. We cannot avoid the issue by arguing that it is a lesser matter and that we should be focusing on big issues such as their relationship with God (I agree that that is the most important issue), their studies and their behavior (also important). Regrettably, money, and the material things that flow from it, tend to overwhelm us all so we need to learn how to cope with money from an early age. Proverbs 22:6 teaches, "Train up a child in the way he should go; even when he is old he will not depart from it."

Ephesians 6:4 actually starts off, "Fathers, do not provoke your children to anger," or, in the NIV, "do not exasperate" them. I can think of few areas where the two principles stated in Ephesians 6:4 are more in conflict than in the matter of how much money to make available to children. Only recently, my eldest daughter told me of her frustration (I do not recall that she said she was "exasperated") that her allowance was never sufficient for her to buy a single major item of clothing without having to save for at least two months. I do not apologize for this approach, and neither am I alone. According to the Forbes list, the two richest men in the world at the time of writing are Warren Buffet and Bill Gates. I recently watched a public interview with them in which they were asked how they passed money on to their children. Bill Gates said something along the lines that his young children had to save up for more than one week to afford the little luxuries that they bought for themselves. When Warren Buffet was asked why he was not leaving all his massive estate to his children, he answered that he had given them what most children do not get, namely an excellent education. However much we love our children and desire to spoil them, giving them unlimited access to funds will indeed "spoil" them.

So how do we teach our children how to handle money? By giving them an allowance which they are allowed to spend more or less as they choose. They will make mistakes, but that is precisely how we all learn, often too late. So let them learn when the mistakes are small—in other words, the sooner the better.

As with all training, I suggest a phased approach in which they learn how to handle increasing amounts as they grow older. When they become teenagers, introduce a step change by which they are obliged to take care of a much larger portion of their personal budgets. The biblical principle of being "faithful over a little; I will set you over much" (Matt. 25:21) is also to be applied to the training of your children.

The key lesson children should learn about money is that no resources are unlimited and expenditure will, of necessity, have to be prioritized. Perhaps if everyone had learned this lesson in childhood we would have adults (even governments) who spent within their means! As the children grow older, they should also be encouraged to work to supplement their incomes. Tasks around the house should be offered to them, and even work for neighbors, friends and acquaintances. Once the law permits it, children should be encouraged to find paid part-time work.

What about loans? I trust that by now you have noticed that I am not keen on debt. The major purpose of my approach to pocket money and children's allowances is *training*. Therefore, make sure you *train* your children to dislike debt. Certainly, you should not make it easy for them, so in general the answer to our question must be "no." Debt is generally intended as fulfillment of our *cultural desire for instant gratification*. We do not wait until we have saved enough but *first buy* what we want and *then pay off* the loan. Are there exceptions? Certainly, but they should meet strict criteria which should be taught so that in later life your children will make wise choices. As with adults, borrowing for educational purposes may be legitimate because the sooner you develop skills, the better. Children are unlikely to get into desperate situations so that exception may not apply, but I am sure a few other situations may justify a loan from parents. Even then, however, a clear repayment scheme must be determined and care taken to make sure the loan is repaid.

Surely, however, you should teach your children to *save*. I was asked by one of my enterprising grandchildren if I would match his contributions to a long-term savings scheme. My wife and I have subsequently set up two schemes available to all our grandchildren, one long term (i.e. available for setting up a home or for a house purchase etc.) and the other medium term. Here is how they work.

For the long-term scheme, we contribute on a 1:1 basis, but the savings can only be accessed after the children have obtained a college degree or completed some tertiary training. The funds are intended for some long-term asset, such as a house, or to set up home. We give the children the information that is set out in Chapter 11 of this book and encourage them to invest in an equity-linked portfolio. Once anything has been drawn from the savings account, our contributions stop. The other scheme is medium term and we add only 50 percent to the children's contributions. They may not draw from the scheme earlier than twenty-four months after the last subsidized contribution has been made. Once anything is drawn, we stop our contributions. We were surprised to discover that one grandchild had already saved $3,500, and another, a thirteen-year-old, had saved $1,700. They quickly switched to new accounts and claimed the subsidies. We readily concurred because we were rewarding them for doing something good in the past.

Stage 1: Early childhood to twelve years old

During their early years, children will probably expect their parents to provide most of what they need. They have no pressing interest in making many of the expenditure decisions which become important to teenagers and beyond. Consequently, during this phase of their development I suggest that parents pay for all normal expenses and only pay a regular but increasing allowance as "pocket money" each week or month.

This pocket money may be freely used for those extras or luxuries which children should learn to provide for themselves. Children also love to give their parents and siblings gifts on special occasions and they should be encouraged to do so from these funds. They should also learn to save on a regular basis, and some means should be provided for them to do so. This could be in the form of the common "piggy bank" or a bank account, or it could be by using one of the special machines called an ABC Learning Bank available from Crown Financial Ministries and designed to teach children.[1] The machine resembles an ATM. It acts as a piggy bank and holds the cash but has a separate slot for a tithe and another for savings. A plastic withdrawal card is provided which resembles a debit card. The card has to be used to withdraw cash. This device teaches children that the only money that can be withdrawn from an ATM is that which has been saved in advance.

I have assumed that you will be teaching your children to tithe. I have always practiced tithing, even though I stop short of being legalistic about it. I therefore think that it is good practice to teach children to tithe from the earliest age. During the latter part of the nineteenth century, the richest man in the world was American industrialist John D. Rockefeller (it has been estimated that if he lived today and we adjusted his net worth by inflation since his death, he would be richer than the three richest men living today *added together*!). What is not well known about Rockefeller was that he was a Christian and he lived frugally and carefully most of his life. He brought his children up so frugally that none of them even guessed that they were rich. He gave each child an allowance each week and made them account for every cent before they received their next allowance. Part of the required accounting was the tithe. He understood the importance of teaching children financial discipline and giving to the Lord's work on a regular basis. This is not a bad example to follow.

How much pocket money or allowance should be given? This is a very personal matter and will have to be determined by each family and take into account where the family lives and the size of the family income. Notice that I deliberately avoid saying that it should take into account *what other children get*. Teach your children from an early age that it is not a good idea to aspire to keep up with the neighbors. Certainly, it should not be a *part* of what we teach them. I suspect that my children always got less than most of their friends because from time to time I heard rumblings, all of which I ignored! Oddly enough, the children who got more than my children were often from poorer homes, where higher allowances simply could not be justified. Parents who are struggling financially sometimes try to compensate by giving large allowances and they forgo the opportunity of using austerity as an excellent means of training their children. Rich or poor, do not give your children more than is necessary. This has little to do with affordability and everything to do with training.

In order to allow for different currencies and different family standards, Table 1 (on page 98) sets out a suggested range of allowances on a *unit* basis. Families can then translate these units into their country's currency and as appropriate to their circumstances. My son who lives in South Africa suggests that multiplying each unit by five gives the correct amount in rands per week. This would translate to a multiplier of about 0.6 to yield a US dollar amount per week (or multiply by 2.5 to yield a monthly amount). My children who live in the USA confirm that this is about what they pay. Probably the same factor would be appropriate for conversion to pounds sterling, as the cost of living is much higher in the UK than in the USA. Readers in other countries will need to work out a factor for themselves. The allowances can be doubled in the months in which the family goes on its annual vacation. The best commendation I can give for this method is that all my children use it, even though we probably kept them short during their training!

I originally set this table up using MS Excel and anyone with my knowledge of Excel (which is modest) can do the same in about half an hour. If you cannot do it, rest assured that your eleven-year-old will be happy to do it for you! (Alternatively, you can download it from the Day One Web site.[2])

Let me illustrate how to use the table.

Firstly, this table assumes that each year a child should be given 15 percent more than he or she received in the previous year. You may choose to make that a different percentage, but 15 percent is generally believed in remuneration theory to be the minimum amount which is "noticeable." The table also assumes an inflation value of 5 percent p.a. which is fixed over the period, although in practice this may differ from year to year and also from country to country. If you set up your spreadsheet correctly, both of these figures can be changed each year if necessary.

Assume you have two children who enter the allowance scheme in the base year. One is four years old and the other is eleven. The four-year-old will start off with an allowance of 1.00 unit per month (or week), and the eleven-year-old will start off with an allowance of 2.66 units. After one

Annual increments 15% p.a. Inflation 5% p.a.

Child's age	4	5	6	7	8	9	10	11	12
Allowance in base year	1.00	1.15	1.32	1.52	1.75	2.01	2.31	2.66	3.06
Allowance in base year plus 1	1.05	1.21	1.39	1.60	1.84	2.11	2.43	2.79	3.21
Allowance in base year plus 2	1.10	1.27	1.46	1.68	1.93	2.22	2.55	2.93	3.37
Allowance in base year plus 3	1.16	1.33	1.53	1.76	2.02	2.33	2.68	3.08	3.54
Allowance in base year plus 4	1.22	1.40	1.61	1.85	2.13	2.44	2.81	3.23	3.72
Allowance in base year plus 5	1.28	1.47	1.69	1.94	2.23	2.57	2.95	3.39	3.90
Allowance in base year plus 6	1.34	1.54	1.77	2.04	2.34	2.70	3.10	3.56	4.10
Allowance in base year plus 7	1.41	1.62	1.86	2.14	2.46	2.83	3.25	3.74	4.30
Allowance in base year plus 8	1.48	1.70	1.95	2.25	2.58	2.97	3.42	3.93	4.52

Table 1: Early childhood to twelve-year-old allowances

year, the four-year-old will get 15 percent more, taking him or her to 1.15 units, but he or she will also get the inflation increase, which will give him or her 1.21 units, as can be seen by following the shaded diagonal line downwards to the right. When this four-year-old reaches twelve, he or she will get 4.52 units. The eleven-year-old sibling will likewise go from 2.66 to 3.21 units, following the darkly shaded diagonal line. Now, assume that in this, the second year, another four-year-old sibling joins the scheme. He or she will start at 1.05 and will then follow the diagonal line below the lightly shaded line—that is, 1.27, 1.53 and so on. This table can be used for all children between the ages of four and twelve.

Stage 2: The teenage years

At the age of about thirteen, children will want to take on additional responsibility for their lives and should be encouraged to do so. My suggestion is that parents should now pay only for normal living expenses plus all education expenses (including uniforms, if applicable) and perhaps for one winter and one summer sport (including any clothing), plus one cultural activity, such as music lessons. Parents should determine and record what these activities are. All the following should then become the responsibility of the teenagers and paid out of their allowances: additional sport; additional cultural activities; nonessential toiletries (e.g. make-up for girls); clothing other than any sports gear included in the parents' portion; all entertainment; mobile phone; candy and all "treat food"; camps or other field trips which are not part of normal education; gifts; pocket money. The teenagers should be given allowances *just sufficient* to cover a reasonable combination of these expenses if they are careful and responsible. They must learn to prioritize and accept that none of us has either the money or the time to do everything all at the same time. Clearly, many gray areas will need to be decided upon. The key is to write everything down and then resist a monthly renegotiation! My wife and I never departed from the scheme, and, because their allowances were low compared with those of their friends, our children all found ways to supplement their incomes.

During the teenage years, the law usually permits part-time paid work to supplement income. All teenagers should be encouraged to take on some weekend or evening work. In some parts of the world, such as the USA, this is within the culture, but in others, such as the UK, it is not. This is a pity, because work is the basis of the biblical economy, and the sooner this is learned, the better. In all cultures, many opportunities will arise if children are encouraged to look for them. If you give them an excessive allowance, you will stifle any such quest.

I may mention that my parents did not believe in giving me and my siblings anything on a regular basis and so, by my final year at school, I was making as much money as most adults earned. I never felt cheated or hard done by, but simply went out and made up for my lack of pocket money. Regrettably, many societies put the onus on governments to provide for our children. There is nothing about this found in the Bible!

Once children move on to college, they will need new amounts and the schemes, in a sense, get simpler. If they leave home and "live in" at college, all living expenses will be dealt with through scholarships or student loans, or through lump sums from you. When our daughters left home to attend college, we extrapolated the scheme for teenagers but increased the sum by a factor. This is because a college student will inevitably have to pay for items such as soap and laundry which come "free" at home. But keep the amount "frugal."

Table 2 suggests allowances that can be applied to teenagers or young people until they commence work. During their college years away from home, increase the allowance by multiplying each unit by a further factor before converting it to the applicable currency. The value of a unit for a teenager will be several times the value of a unit for an under-twelve-year-old child. A good starting point may be a factor of ten times the early childhood unit; this table has been produced on that assumption. Once again, set up your spreadsheet as I have done, so that this multiplying factor can be used as a parameter to drive the entire worksheet. In all probability, the years from age nineteen onwards will be spent at college, where a further multiplying factor of 1.5 to 2.0 may be appropriate.

Training in planning and budgeting

Use every opportunity to include your children in planning and budgeting. Our two sons showed a great deal of interest in accounting from the age of

Training your children: pocket money and allowances

Annual increments 15% p.a. Inflation 5% p.a.
Teen factor 10.   **College factor 1.5**

Teenager's age	13	14	15	16	17	18	19	20	21
Allowance in base year	10.00	11.50	13.23	15.21	17.49	20.11	34.70	39.90	45.89
Allowance in base year plus 1	10.50	12.08	13.89	15.97	18.36	21.12	36.43	41.90	48.18
Allowance in base year plus 2	11.03	12.68	14.58	16.77	19.28	22.18	38.25	43.99	50.59
Allowance in base year plus 3	11.58	13.31	15.31	17.61	20.25	23.28	40.16	46.19	53.12
Allowance in base year plus 4	12.16	13.98	16.08	18.49	21.26	24.45	42.17	48.50	55.77
Allowance in base year plus 5	12.76	14.68	16.88	19.41	22.32	25.67	44.28	50.92	58.56
Allowance in base year plus 6	13.40	15.41	17.72	20.38	23.44	26.95	46.50	53.47	61.49
Allowance in base year plus 7	14.07	16.18	18.61	21.40	24.61	28.30	48.82	56.14	64.57
Allowance in base year plus 8	14.77	16.99	19.54	22.47	25.84	29.72	51.26	58.95	67.79

Table 2: Teenage allowances

about ten. We therefore encouraged them to participate both in our domestic budget as well as in controlling the finances. Our youngest son was a hard taskmaster. As mentioned in Chapter 4, he would join my wife shopping at the supermarket and, if he considered purchasing an item to be poor stewardship or outside the budget, he would remove it from the shopping basket and return it to the shelves. Imagine my wife's frustration!

We were fortunate in that, as a family, we traveled frequently, mostly in Europe and the USA. We always divided the planning and financial-control tasks among the four children on a rotation basis. One would get the job of researching places to visit, one would plan our itinerary, one would have to compile a budget, one would have to take a video and another take photos. The budget would be done on accounting stationery, allowing the "trip accountant" to compare actual expenditure at the end of each day with the budget (in later years, we took along a laptop computer). This had its own frustrations, forcing us at times to eat hamburgers or sleep in a budget motel for days in order to get back to budget! Likewise, the planning was very detailed. I can remember being ordered off an interstate highway and being directed to a shopping mall because the plan called for a "comfort break" whether any of us needed one or not! This training did them all good, however, as they all ended up in management jobs and both our sons became chief executives at an early age. I have included a model travel budget in Appendix 3. This can also be downloaded from the Day One Web site.[3]

Rearing children is a serious responsibility, and the aspects dealt with in this chapter are only one facet. I strongly recommend that alongside this chapter you read and apply some of the excellent books on bringing up children that I recommended in Chapter 1.

Notes

1 ABC Learning Bank, in the "Children's Resources" section at: crown.org.

2 See note 6 in Chapter 1.

3 As above.

Conclusion

The Bible is not silent on the matter of finance. It requires us neither to live the life of a recluse nor to merely exist, but to enjoy all that God has given us. However, we are not to make idols of God's blessings.

As in all matters, we must evaluate the worldview that dominates secular thinking and check to see where and to what degree this differs from how things ought to be as set out in the Bible. We cannot simply follow the wisdom of this world by joining the materialistic, debt-ridden, pleasure-seeking world in which we live. Instead, we must be faithful stewards of all that God has entrusted to us, enjoy his blessings with thanksgiving, be generous, especially in providing for the poor, save and avoid debt. In doing these things we may well end up *rich*, but, more importantly, we must end up being *content*.

Resources for further help

Kelvin Worthington, *Right on the Money* (Fearn: Christian Focus, 2009)

Quicken Personal Finance Software; visit: www.quicken.intuit.com

For downloadable Microsoft Excel spreadsheets, including ones for special occasions such as weddings, visit: www.spreadsheet123.com.

For a range of resources, visit: www.crownmoneymap.org; www.daveramsey.com; or www.mint.com

Many banks offer their own financial-planning software that links in directly with your bank and credit card accounts. Check this with your bank.

Schedule of current assets and liabilities

Many banks offer their own financial-planning software that links in directly with your bank and credit card accounts. Check this with your bank.

Values must be "fair market value", i.e. what you could get in a realistic sale of the asset
Complete one for all members of the household, then sum for the family's assets

Assets (what you own)	
House or houses	
Less outstanding value of mortgage(s)	
Your "equity" in your house(s)	
Other Assets	
Cash in bank	
Savings	
Stocks and bonds or other investments	
Cash value of insurance policies	
Cash value of provision for pension	
Value of secure loans made *to* others	
Car(s)	
Houshold effects (furniture etc.)	
Jewelry	
Other personal goods, e.g. cameras, computers*	
Value of any collection, e.g. stamps	
Total Assets	
Liabilities (what you owe, apart from mortgages listed above)	
Outstanding value of loan on car(s)	
Outstanding value of any loan on household goods or other property	
Bank overdraft	
Credit card debt	
Personal loans from any institution	
Personal loans from any person	
Student loans for which you have accepted responsibility	
Any other loans or amount for which you are responsible	
Total Liabilities	
Net Assets or, if —, ** **net Liabilities** (Total Assets less Total Liabilities)	

*Items such as clothing have little or no value as they cannot be converted into cash
**If negative, you have too many loans and need to make radical changes to repay debts in as short a period as possible.

Spreadsheet available from Day One Web site: (UK) www.dayone.co.uk; (US) www.dayonebookstore.com

Model household budget

	Jan Budget	Jan Actual	>>>>>>>>	Dec Budget	Dec Actual	Annual Budget	Annual Actual	Variance
Income Budget						If annual known, complete this column first and then divide by 12 and fill in each month		
Gross Salary(ies)								
Interest income								
Other income								
Less Income Tax, social security, etc.								
Net Spendable Income								
Spending Budget								
Non-discretionary Expenditure								
Giving to the Lord's work								
Accommodation costs								
Mortgage or rent								
Property taxes (rates)								
Insurance								
Electricity								
Gas						*For annual payments, complete this column first and then divide by 12 and fill in each month		
Water and sanitation								
Refuse collection								
Maintenance								
Garden/yard								
Food and toiletries								
Supermarket								
Other								
Insurance								
Life								
Health								
Disability								
Medical and dental costs								
Medicines								
Debt redemption*								
Clothing [create a separate line for each family member]								
Education								
School fees								
Books and materials								
Sports equipment								
Sports and/or cultural tuition/fees								
School clothing/uniforms								
Day care/nursery school								

Spreadsheet available from Day One Web site: (UK) www.dayone.co.uk; (US) www.dayonebookstore.com

For annual payments, complete this column first and then divide by 12 and fill in each month

Discretionary Expenditure

Entertainment
TV/DVDs/CDs
Movies/theatre/sports-viewing
Sport
Eating out
Magazines/newspapers etc.
Babysitters
Outings
Pets
Special occasions, e.g. Christmas*
Saving for vacations
Clubs and societies

Transportation
Car(s) payments (if any)
Car replacement savings*
Road tax/licences
Insurance
Petrol (gas) and oil
Maintenance*
Tires*
Public transport

Telephone and Internet

Capital Items
One-off cost if cash paid (good)
Monthly payment if on credit (bad!)

Miscellaneous
Hair and beauty
Birthday gifts*
Christmas gifts*
Other gifts
Children's allowances [best to create a separate line for each child]
Husband and wife allowances (for their own discretionary expenditure)
Unforeseen (say 5% of actual expenditure)

Savings (only after all short-term debts have been fully paid)*

Total Spending

Surplus/shortfall on Income (Spendable Income less Total Expenditure)

*All these items and others paid annually should be budgeted on an annual basis and one twelfth put into savings each month. Use this as a guide; each family should set up its own list of budget items to suit its needs.

Spreadsheet available from Day One Web site: (UK) www.dayone.co.uk; (US) www.dayonebookstore.com

Model travel budget

	Budget	Actual	Cumulative Budget	Cumulative Actual	Variance
One-off costs					
Prepaid accommodation					
Prepaid auto rental					
Other one-offs					
Total pre-holiday expenses in home currency					
Country 1	Rate of Exchange:				
Day 1					
Accommodation					
Travel (gas, rail, bus, etc.)					
Meals					
Breakfast					
Lunch					
Dinner					
Attractions/excursions					
Gifts					
Day 1 Totals					
Day 2					
Accommodation					
Travel (gas, rail, bus, etc.)					
Meals					
Breakfast					
Lunch					
Dinner					
Attractions/excursions					
Gifts					
Day 2 Totals					

Spreadsheet available from Day One Web site: (UK) www.dayone.co.uk; (US) www.dayonebookstore.com

Day 3						
Accommodation						
Travel (gas, rail, bus, etc.)						
Meals						
Breakfast						
Lunch						
Dinner						
Attractions/excursions						
Gifts						
Day 3 Totals						
*Day 4, 5, 6 ... Day n.						
Grand Totals Country 1, local currency						
Grand Totals, Country 1, home currency						
Country 2	Rate of Exchange:					
Continue from Day n+1						
*Details as before						
Grand Totals Country 2, local currency						
Grand Totals, Country 2, home currency						
Repeat for each country to be visited						
Total entire trip in home currency						
*Repeat Day budget for each country visited.						

Spreadsheet available from Day One Web site: (UK) www.dayone.co.uk; (US) www.dayonebookstore.com

About Day One:

Day One's threefold commitment:

- To be faithful to the Bible, God's inerrant, infallible Word;
- To be relevant to our modern generation;
- To be excellent in our publication standards.

I continue to be thankful for the publications of Day One. They are biblical; they have sound theology; and they are relative to the issues at hand. The material is condensed and manageable while, at the same time, being complete—a challenging balance to find. We are happy in our ministry to make use of these excellent publications.

JOHN MACARTHUR, PASTOR-TEACHER, GRACE COMMUNITY CHURCH, CALIFORNIA

It is a great encouragement to see Day One making such excellent progress. Their publications are always biblical, accessible and attractively produced, with no compromise on quality. Long may their progress continue and increase!

JOHN BLANCHARD, AUTHOR, EVANGELIST AND APOLOGIST

Visit our website for more information and to request a free catalogue of our books.

In the UK: www.dayone.co.uk
In North America: www.dayonebookstore.com

JOHN TEMPLE

PAPERBACK, 96PP

978-1-84625-150-4

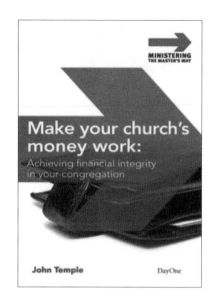

The finances of a church are a concrete expression of its vision, its priorities and its commitment to doing things 'decently and in order'. This book examines the basis of sound biblical stewardship as applied to the practical aspects of budgeting, reporting and control of expenses in a church. It suggests a remuneration policy for pastors and other paid workers, outlines the responsibilities of members in supporting their church and includes a suggested spreadsheet for budgeting and reporting. Written in non-accountancy terminology, this book should be read by church leaders and anyone who spends any of the church's money, as well as by all who give money to a local church.

Dr. John Temple spent his secular career as an entrepreneur and businessman, mostly at Chief Executive level. He is therefore well qualified to deal with financial and accounting matters. He has held virtually every office in a church, from youth leader to deacon and elder, church secretary and treasurer. Throughout this service, he sought to teach and apply sound theology to the policy of the church in financial and administrative matters. He helped plant four churches. He holds a Ph.D., a B.Sc. (Eng.) and an AEP (MBA equivalent). John and his wife Yvonne live in the New Forest in Hampshire, England.

A failure to establish biblically derived financial policies and practices often leads churches into trouble. Following this eminently practical guide should ensure that both God and his servants are honoured in this vital area and that much potential difficulty and heartache are avoided. Supremely qualified to write on this subject, John Temple is a peerless conveyor of sanctified common sense. I heartily commend this little volume.

JONATHAN STEPHEN, DIRECTOR, AFFINITY, AND PRINCIPAL, WEST (WALES EVANGELICAL SCHOOL OF THEOLOGY)

Be successful; be spiritual—
How to serve God in the workplace

JOHN TEMPLE

PAPERBACK, 176PP

978–1–84625–109–2

How does a Christian live out his faith on a '24/7'
basis? How do Christians glorify God through
their lives, pointing others to Christ? This
requires a Christian world view that governs the
economy and the Christian's behaviour at work.
How do Christian managers fulfil their
responsibilities? Do they accept current secular
views taught at the business schools? How are
public companies to be run? What about pension?
How do Christians deal with stress and problems
in their jobs? What is a Christian's attitude to
wealth? These are all essential elements of a
Christian world view for our jobs.

John Temple　　　　　　DayOne

Be successful; be spiritual! is a thorough
study of the biblical principles underlying all
of work and business. Everyone, from the
person just entering the work force to the
experienced CEO, will find valuable Biblical
guidance in this book.
—*Jerry Bridges, Author, The Pursuit of Holiness*

This book will show countless people that
true success has a sound spiritual basis and I
warmly commend it.
—*John Blanchard*